A Brighter Sun

Samuel Selvon

Longman Drumbeat

Longman Group Limited
Longman House, Burnt Mill,
Harlow, Essex CM20 2JE, England
and Associated Companies throughout the World

First published by Alan Wingate 1952
First published in Longman Drumbeat 1979
Fourth impression 1983

ISBN 0 582 64265.5

Printed in Hong Kong by
Sheck Wah Tong Printing Press Ltd

To my mother
and father

A BRIGHTER SUN

CHAPTER ONE

On New Year's Day, 1939, while Trinidadians who had money or hopes of winning money were attending the races in the Queen's Park Savannah, Port of Spain, a number of Jewish refugees fleeing Nazi persecution in Europe landed on the island. There was an almost instant increase in the rental of residences and business places, and later more refugees were refused entrance. A development plan costing $14,000,000 was approved by the Secretary of State for the Colonies but nipped in the bud when war was declared. In April, when pouis blossomed and keskidees sang for rain, local forces were mobilized. In May a German training ship with a crew of 270 paid a visit. Emergency regulations were introduced, mail and telegrams censored, the churches prayed for peace, and the adjacent territorial waters were proclaimed a prohibited area. A man went about the streets of the city riding a bicycle and balancing a bottle of rum on his head. An East Indian, reputedly mad, walked to the wharf and dipped a key in the sea and went away muttering to himself. A big burly Negro called Mussolini, one-legged and arrogant, chased a small boy who was teasing him and fell down, cursing loudly, much to the amusement of passers-by. In September much rain fell; it was the middle of the rainy season. Usually it is Indian summer weather—the natives call it *petite carème*—lasting for a month. It is the best time for planting crops. War was declared and measures necessary for the preservation of internal order were intensified, and wartime regulations brought into force.

All activities concentrated on the "war effort" in 1940. Money collected in various ways was sent to England. Six young men from the Air Training Scheme left to join the R.A.F. Negotiations between England and America for bases in the island came to a head when a United States major discussed the actual locations of the proposed bases with the governor. Air-raid precautions were introduced. French residents pledged their support to General de Gaulle, and a man named Lafeet died in a hut far in the hills of the Northern Range, and nobody knew anything until three weeks later. A model township was opened on the outskirts of the city to relieve the housing shortage. Land was rented to the peasantry in a "grow more food" campaign. Teachers' salaries were increased and two buses placed at the disposal of schoolchildren to convey them from remote places to the handicraft and housecraft centres. The biggest budget in the history of the colony was passed. There were thirty-six strikes. Sugar and banana industries declined; the drop in sugar was the worst in four years.

In Chaguanas, a sugar-cane district halfway down the western coast of the island, the biggest thing to happen, bigger even than the war, was Tiger's wedding. The whole village turned up for it, Negro and Indian alike, for when Indian people got married it was a big thing, plenty food and drink, plenty ceremony.

Tiger didn't know anything about the wedding until his father told him. He didn't even know the girl. But he bowed to his parents' wishes. He was only sixteen years old and was not in the habit of attending Indian ceremonies in the village.

But he knew a little about weddings, that Indians were married at an early age, and that after the ceremony friends and relatives would bring him gifts until he began to eat; only then would they stop the offerings.

Every night and every morning for a week close relatives came and rubbed him down to prepare his body for married life. On the morning of the wedding he bathed. They dressed him in the wedding gown and put a crown on his head. His father said, "Boy, dese people not so rich, so don't stayam too long to eat."

At the back of the bride's house a great tent of bamboo and coconut branches had been erected. Five goats and six sheep had been slaughtered, an extravagance which could be afforded only at a time like this.

Tiger looked at everybody and everything with a tight feeling in his throat. He wished he knew more about what was going to happen to him.

As part of the ceremony he had to rub a red powder through the path in the middle of her head when a white sheet was thrown over them. As he did this he lifted the veil and looked at her face. She must have been about his age. She had black, sad eyes, long hair, undeveloped breasts.

"What you name?" he asked breathlessly.

"Urmilla," she whispered timidly.

Tiger didn't think that he would have to look at that face for the rest of his life. The whole affair had been arranged for him; he didn't have anything to do with it. He wondered if she could cook, but he didn't ask himself if she knew anything about what boys and girls did when they got married, because he didn't know either. He was aware of a painful exhilaration; painful because neither of them understood, exhilarating because it was something different in his monotonous life.

They offered him a cow and a hut in Barataria and two

hundred dollars in cash, besides smaller things. He didn't know where Barataria was. He didn't know what to expect, or whether he should wait for more gifts before beginning the feast. And then on a sudden impulse—perhaps it was fear, uncertainty—he took up a piece of *meetai* and bit it. That ended the offerings.

Afterwards his father caught him alone for a minute and hissed, "Yuh fool! Could have gettam plenty more thing! Yuh eatam too quick, stupid boy!"

But it didn't matter to Tiger. Vaguely, like morning mist, he found himself wondering what life was going to be like.

As was the custom, the bride had to spend three days at his home, then they would spend three days at her family's. After that, they could go and live in their own house.

When Tiger had handed Urmilla over to his mother, all the boys and girls from the neighbourhood came up and started to call out to him.

"Tiger! So yuh married now!"

"Yuh is a big man now, boy!"

Some of the older folk drove them away, but Tiger would have liked for them to come. He was familiar with them, he could make jokes and talk. But now he was a man. He would have to learn to be a man, he would have to forget his friends. After all, he thought, they still little children!

In the next three days his mind was in a turmoil. He went out into the canefields where he had toiled with his father and brothers. Wind blew strongly here: he liked to lift his head and smell burned cane. What had life been for him? Days in the fields, evenings playing with other children, roti and *aloo* in the night. Sometimes they sang songs. His father had a drum, and when it was Saturday night the neighbours came and they drank and sang. And now all that was gone. He felt a tremendous responsibility falling on his shoulders. He tried not to think about it.

The third day his mind was in a riotous fever. He sat in the yard under a mango tree with Ramlal, an old Indian who often consoled him when he was beaten by his father or mother.

"What I must do?" he asked Ramlal, and Ramlal laughed.

"Is how yuh mean, boy?"

"I mean—I don't know what to do when I go with the girl."

"What, boy! Never seeam your *bap* and *mai* when dey sleeping in de night?"

"Yes, but—"

"Well, is dat self. You doam same thing. You gettam house which side Barataria, gettam land, cow—well, you go live dat side. Haveam plenty boy chile—girl chile no good, only bring trouble on yuh head. You live dat side, plantam garden, live good."

In those few words Ramlal summed up things for Tiger. But he didn't feel any sexual excitement at the thought of being alone with Urmilla. Even when he had looked at her face under the *purdah*—the white sheet thrown over them— for to him everything was a whirling, swift event, in which he was told to do this, and do that, and he obeyed.

The last three days at Urmilla's parents he was glad for this putting off of the unknown, this stretching of the few days before the overwhelming river burst over its banks and swept him off his immature feet.

The village of Barataria is situated about four miles east of the capital Port of Spain. Most of it lay on the southern side of the Eastern Main Road, until the war started and people began to look for places to live, the city being overcrowded with servicemen and jobseekers. House owners in the city put a few sticks of furniture in their rooms and charged exorbitant rents for "furnished" apartments. Crafty men advertised themselves as house agents who could get you a house for a small fee. Once involved, it was a matter of paying small amounts from time to time, and when at last you saw the house you either didn't like it or had to pay a year's rent in advance. One Negro British Guianese did so well that he opened an office and advertised widely. In three months' time he had a staff of three and was extending business to cover secondhand miscellany. In six months he had a car; by the time the government decided to put up a rent tribunal he had built two houses and had a thousand dollars put away in the bank.

The private estate that owned Barataria leased lots to enterprising housebuilders. In a short time bungalows were going up, to be bought or rented before completion. Roads were laid out, starting a little north of the main road, to run through the village for about half a mile. The railroad connecting other districts to the capital ran parallel to the main road, about one hundred yards south of it. Some of the roads crossed the railway lines. There were ten, running north to south. Then there were thirteen, running across these east to west. The down roads were called avenues, and numbered from one to ten. The cross ones were called streets, and numbered from one to thirteen. The roads were built roughly, with rocks and stones. If a taxi driver was asked to leave the main road and enter the village he said, "Who, me? My car on dem macadam and big stone? Not me, papa!" In the rainy season puddles of water and mud made the village just like the Laventille Swamp which bordered the western side of the area. The drains were never completely dry, as the land was level and drainage difficult. Mosquitoes bred by the thousands and frogs croaked the night away. Gardeners who had been living in Barataria before the house hunt started remained in the back streets, near twelfth and thirteenth streets, still living in their thatched huts. Most of them were East Indians. The concrete bungalows near the railway and main road went to middle-class families of various nationalities.

First man to put up a shop was a Chinese. It was at the corner of sixth street and sixth avenue, about the busiest spot in the village. Another opened a laundry. At the corner of sixth avenue and the main road, a good business spot because local trains halted there, shops—groceries, parlours, sweetshops, barber saloons—and general trade opened up. An Indian woman put a table with a coal-pot on the sidewalk and made roti to sell with curried potatoes at twelve cents apiece. With beef or mutton it was a shilling. An ice company put an icebox and a scale, selling ice at a penny a pound and snowball— shaved ice with syrup and condensed milk—from four to six cents. If you only had a penny you could get a "press"—the shaved ice was rammed into a small aluminum cup and taken out and dipped in syrup.

The main road streamed with traffic all day and night. Those who worked in the city could wait at the halt for a train or catch a bus or a taxi on the main road, arriving at their place of work in ten or fifteen minutes' time. The main road itself was wide and asphalted, with sidewalks. Between seventh and eighth avenues a concrete bridge with iron rails spanned a small river. In the wet season the river ran under another bridge fifty yards from the main road, in tenth avenue, and emptied itself in the swamp. Villagers called the bridge on the main road Jumbie Bridge because they were superstitious about it. They said that every year an accident was bound to happen there.

The village was almost as cosmopolitan as the city. Indians and Negroes were in the majority. In the back streets the Indians lived simply, observing their customs and tending their fields, bringing the produce to sell in sixth avenue or going to the market in San Juan, a town bordering the eastern side. The earth was black and rich; they grew vegetables in the yard, kept a few chickens and perhaps a few cattle or a donkey. The Negroes were never farmers, and most of them did odd jobs in the village or the city. But it didn't need any knowledge of farming to dig a hole and put in tomato seeds; the land was so rich that nearly every villager grew peppers or bananas or string beans.

The government erected a school on sixth avenue; many children used to run away and hunt crabs or cascadura fish in the swamp instead of attending. Opposite the school was a large savannah on which cattle and donkeys grazed and children played. Anything would do for a bat and ball to play cricket. A coconut-palm branch, properly cut and shaped, made an excellent bat; fruit seeds, empty tin cans, even stones, served as an inexhaustible stock of balls.

So the people poured from the overfilled city, and though they grumbled at the mosquitoes and the stones in the streets on which they "stumped" their toes, others followed them, filling up the area, which was not even a mile long or half a mile wide.

It was evening time when Tiger and Urmilla arrived in Barataria. A cow moaned in a field. A radio was playing jazz music, jarring on the quietude. Across the level stretch of land on the border of the swamp the sun sank splendidly in a pool of red, saffron, deep purple, and the coconut trees behind the land which Tiger was to rent later cast long, last shadows.

Tiger lit a fire of green bush so that the smoke would drive away the mosquitoes. Then he milked the cow under the rose mango tree. Urmilla watched him from the kitchen window. They had hardly exchanged any words since leaving Chaguanas. They had come to the hut and went about putting things away like two people who did not know each other.

There were two chairs, a small table, and some cooking utensils. The hut was one room. The floor and walls were smooth mud. The roof was thatched with palm leaves. The kitchen was behind and separated from the hut. It was, in fact, a miniature of the hut, except that there was an earthen fireplace, dug in the ground. And it was in a dilapidated condition, leaning to one side.

When Urmilla tried to lift the massala stone with which she would grind curry, she found it was too heavy. She turned shyly to her husband and asked him to lift it for her. It was the first time she had spoken directly to him. She swept the floor with a broom made from the stems of palm leaves, put wood in the fireplace, and went to catch water at the standpipe near the corner of the street.

Later they ate roti and *bigan* in silence. Tiger chewed slowly, tasting the food. At least she could cook, he told himself.

After the meal he sat on the floor with his legs drawn up under him. "Get the cigarettes for me," he commanded.

Urmilla hastened to obey.

Tiger had never smoked. He had only seen his father and the others. But he had decided that he was not going to appear a small boy before his wife. Men smoked: he would smoke. He would drink rum, curse, swear, bully the life out of her if she did not obey him. Hadn't he seen when his father did that? And didn't he know what to do when they went to bed? But he refused to think much about later, in the bed. Unknowingness folded about him so he couldn't breathe. He was afraid.

Urmilla handed him the cigarettes and matches. He pulled one out of the pack, beat the end on the box of matches, and put it between his lips and lit it clumsily and inhaled.

All this time Urmilla was fascinatedly looking at him. And when Tiger began to cough so that his eyes ran water she knew. Ordinarily she would not have dared to laugh. But her emotions were too tightly drawn, like ropes across her breasts. And she felt that if she laughed the tautness would snap and set her free.

It flashed in Tiger's mind that this was rudeness and that he should slap her into respect for him when she laughed. And then the humour of the situation broadened like a ring in a pond and pushed other thoughts out of its path. Tightness in Tiger went as he burst into a fit of laughter. They laughed until they felt less afraid of each other. The joke of the cigarette was just a starter; the rest of their laughter was to drown out uncertainty, the knowledge that they would do something soon which they had never done before. And after they laughed, for the first time the thought gave them a thrill.

Urmilla moved away uneasily; Tiger ground the cigarette in the ground.

That night they slept separately on sugar bags spread on the floor. Tiger crept across the room and huddled up in the corner, afraid of his thoughts and wishing with all his heart that he could fall asleep. Urmilla cried silently in the bags she had folded as a pillow.

When Tiger got up in the morning Urmilla had already milked the cow and was kneading flour. "Good morning," she said shyly, not lifting her head. Tiger smiled but he didn't answer. He went out in the yard and cut a toothbrush from the hibiscus fence. He chewed at the end of the stem and scrubbed his teeth with it when it frazzled out. He dipped a calabash full of water from the barrel at the side of the kitchen and dashed it on his face. The sun was halfway up in the sky.

He decided that he had better begin to talk freely with his

wife. That way she wouldn't know he was doubtful and fearful of the future.

"Now so, Urmilla, what you doing home by you?" he asked when they sat on the floor to breakfast.

Words came tumbling from the girl like water from a burst dam. "Oh, Tiger, I have plenty work to do. Clean the house, cook, go out and graze the cattle—"

"Yes, girl, me too. Plenty things to do by my father house. Every day I go in the fields and work, work. In the evening we play. All the boys and girls come, and we play under the mango tree. I wish I was back home now."

"But, Tiger, we married now! We can't go back to we father and mother house. We have to live here by weself."

Tiger drank tea from a large enamel cup. "Yes, I know that. Don't think I don't know. You must remember, first thing is that I is the man in the house, and you have to obey me."

Urmilla said quickly, "Yes, Tiger."

"Now second thing," he said, "is to get land. We go grow crop and sell. Is San Juan where the estate office is, I going up there now and make arrangement. I don't know the exact spot, but I could always ask somebody."

He caught a bus on the main road, and by then the sun was high in the sky, and the wind warm and constant. It was easy to find the office, everybody in San Juan knew where it was. He signed a contract, marking a big "X" for his name, to rent two lots of land. He was worried about the negotiation; he wished his father or one of his uncles was there with him. But the thought made him ashamed. He was married, and he was a big man now. He might as well learn to do things without the assistance of other people.

When he got back to Barataria it was evening. He dropped off by the corner, and seeing the rumshop open, went in. The same spur which had made him smoke now tickled him to get drunk. Only men got drunk, not boys. He remembered once in Chaguanas his father was drinking in a rumshop and he had to go and bring him home. When his father saw him he said, "Ohe, boy, come an' take ah little one, it go killam all de germs in yuh belly." And he took a little one, urged by his father's companions, and the rum coursed down his throat as if pitchoil had been soaked in his mouth and a match set to it. Then men had laughed loudly when tears sprang to his eyes.

He ordered a drink.

The men in the rumshop, talking and laughing, looked at him briefly. He stood with the glass in his hand and looked around. Acutely conscious that they were not looking at him, he gulped the rum with an effort and chased it with a soda water. He wanted to buck up his courage and say something to show them he was a man, that he could swallow rum just as they did.

But no one cared if Tiger was a man or not.

Warmth travelled over his body. He went to a dirty table around which two young men were sitting. There was a slop pail near and one of them was leaning from his chair and spitting in it.

"You living in Barataria?" Tiger asked.

"Who is you?" one of them demanded. "Why yuh want to find dat out?"

"Is just that I newly come here to live. I don't know the place good yet, man."

"Well, sit down nar," they invited. "Have ah liquor wid we. But you must buy."

It was a chance to prove he was a man. "Call for another bottle on me, man," he said, pulling a bill from his pocket. "All of we is Indian together; let we drink and make merry."

Already he owned land, he boasted to his companions.

He had a house, a cow, a wife. And he thought to himself that he ought to have done it last night, only he couldn't summon up enough courage. Tonight he would show her. Nobody had told him he was still a boy, but they didn't have to speak for him to know.

He got up suddenly from the table. He was feeling giddy. He staggered through the door and he knew they were laughing behind his back, but he didn't care.

Urmilla had lit the kerosene lamp and was waiting anxiously. Through the fog in his brain he could see fear in her eyes.

"Why you stay so long, Tiger?" she asked gladly.

He sulked. He was the man in the house, he could come and go as he pleased. He didn't answer.

They ate in silence. Tiger watched Urmilla out of the corners of his eyes. Now that he had decided to do it, she appeared altogether different. Her hair was glossy in the lamplight, her eyes shining. Almost as if she knew. He wished that he knew more about everything—about planting crops at the right time, about living with a wife, and exactly how to go about the thing. In some way he sensed that unless he did it he would never cease to be a boy, to be treated like a boy.

Later they sat silent. Urmilla shelled pigeon peas she had bought from a passing vender for the next day's lunch.

He watched her. Did he have to tell her first?

They went to bed. For a long time he lay looking at the thatched roof, making up his mind. Then quietly, like he was stalking a deer, he drew his bags near to his bride.

Urmilla moved and opened her eyes. She knew what was going to happen and she tried not to be afraid. Her mother had said, "*Beti*, whatever happen, don't frighten. You is a woman now."

It was the same thing with Urmilla: she felt she had to prove herself a woman in front of Tiger.

Young passion burst and swept them so they didn't know really what they were doing. If Tiger had known that this powerful force was going to grip him so that he wouldn't be afraid, it would have been so easy for him to let himself die and switch on the force. Because afterwards he was aware that he of his own accord had taken no part in the thing. A great desire for his wife had come over him, possessing his brain.

Before they fell asleep in each other's arms he told himself that the next time he would just die and let the power do its work.

And the next morning they lay lazily on the bags on the floor, looking at each other with the wonder of the new knowledge.

And they did it again.

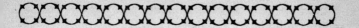

CHAPTER TWO

There was a change in the economic and social life and outlook
of Trinidadians in 1941. United States personnel arrived, and
the construction of bases provided work at high wages—higher
than anyone had ever worked for before. Clerks quit their
desks and papers and headed for the bases, farmers left the
land untilled, labourers deserted the oil and sugar industries
in the south, there was a rush to where the money flowed.
From neighbouring islands, Grenada, St. Vincent, Barbados,
natives kissed their wives and relatives good-bye and came
to Trinidad to make their fortunes. The city was crammed
as the Yankee dollar lured men away from home and family.
Politically a new constitution came into force, increasing
the number of elected members to the Legislative Council
by two and reducing the strength of official representation
from nine to three. At the end of March the Stars and Stripes
waved over Trinidad territory. Acquisition of lands for the
bases left hundreds homeless and posed a problem. Soon after
the arrival of American troops fights began between civilians and servicemen. There was a new scale of increased taxa-
tion "upon those best able to bear it." A man named Afoo
Dayday was caught urinating behind a tree in a park and was
jailed. An Indian man from Gasparillo, a southern village,

went about the city eating bottles and sticking pins and needles in his body. The sum of $791,228 was voted for slum clearance. Imports were controlled, a committee appointed to settle displaced persons, another to assist the Rockefeller Institute of New York in conducting a malaria survey. A housing settlement was opened in the southern district of San Fernando.

How Joe Martin ever came to leave the city of Port of Spain and settle down to a comparatively smooth-flowing life in Barataria with Rita was once history to some people in Trinidad. He himself used to muse on the matter over a bottle of rum, telling Rita, "But, gul, life is a helluva thing, *oui*. But look how Ah take up meself and leave sweetman life in town, look how Ah leave de boys coasting, and come up here to live wid yuh in de bush! But life is a helluva thing, *oui*." Rita, accustomed to his reminiscing, would sneer. "Why yuh don't go back den? Why de hell yuh don't go back to de barrack-yard where yuh born? Ah did always know yuh can't live ah decent life . . ."

In the dry season a stream dies just on the northeastern outskirts of Port of Spain, in a district called St. Anns. It just trickles to nothingness, and the bed is dry and rocky, even becoming covered with green shrubs at the farther end. But in the wet season the stream gathers courage and ventures farther down. To convey this water to the sea, the Dry River —a concrete canal about twenty feet deep with an average width of thirty feet—was built. When the rains come and the stream is swollen the Dry River becomes a swirling current, sweeping the oddest miscellany to the sea. But it is not useless in the dry season. Those who live on its banks find a variety of uses for it. Washers bleach their clothes on its bed, rubbish is toppled over its sides in the night—and in the day when nobody is looking; dead animals rot there unless the water rises to wash them down. Children play in the Dry River, rolling bicycle wheels and barrel hoops or playing "bat and ball." When water is flowing not high enough to be dangerous they play "boat race" with bits of wood. People walking to the central parts of the city use it as a road. Young men gather under the bridges where roads cross to gamble. Steel bands practise there, as the players then consider themselves out of the way. By night the Dry River is a rendezvous for lovers; swift consummations have happened on its hard bed, in places where overhanging trees or houses hide the light of the moon. Because of the scarcity of public conveniences, some find it convenient to slip down and relieve themselves. The Dry River has been known to cause and prevent bloodshed. It has been the frontier line for steel band fights— "If yuh only cross de river is trouble here tonight!" Men have chased their enemies to that border and hesitated to go across. By day, far more by night, people who consider themselves respectable think twice before being seen in the area; if they have friends there they are uneasy about visiting: "But, gul, yuh mean allyuh can't try to get ah better place? Dis area too bad, dey always have fight here." Young men born east of the Dry River, on Rose Hill or Calvary Hill or Laventille, grow up with the understanding that they are slum folk and dangerous people.

George Street runs parallel with the Dry River. It is separated from it by a chain of dwelling and business houses which, viewed from the street, give the impression of being jammed so tightly together that if one was removed the others would collapse through sheer pressure. Behind this, in the narrow alleys between the houses and the barrackyards, the people are so packed that Ma Jones knows what Ma Lambie is cooking for lunch just by poking her head through a crack in the dilapidated wall which separates their kitchens. And when she is going to have a bath: "A-a, but Ma Lambie, Ah ent see yuh bade for a long time now." "Why yuh don't mine yuh own blasted business?" In the night, there is the smell of stale food and rubbish piled high near the pavements. Slinking, mangy dogs sniff and explore the debris for something to eat. Shrunken old people, wrapped in old newspapers and bags, crouch in doorways and on the cold concrete sidewalks. In George Street most anything lies in the drains—coconut shells, tattered clothing, broken bottles from an early battle, empty tin cans, dead dogs. Old women come out in the night and stand or sit on the steps. The way the houses are built, you could walk on the pavement and look through a window and see into bedrooms and dining rooms. The women sit with their babies on their knees and talk to one another, laughing loudly at rude jokes, scratching their legs and backsides. The way they sit, one could see right up: "Wat de hell he looking at? 'E never see—yet?" Many of them cook food to sell. They make souse—boiled pork seasoned with lime and pepper and cucumber—and black pudding. They rest their trays on a barrel or box outside a rumshop. When these places of vantage are already taken—for a brisk trade goes on with the rum drinkers, who like to have pudding or souse while drinking— they sit by the corners or on the pavement. They sell cheaply, because only the poor people buy. On a Saturday night especially some middle- and upper-class families like their souse and black pudding and delegate a member of the family to make the purchase as inconspicuously as possible. The venders also sell bake—a kind of bread—and accra and float— a light bake, with saltfish fried in oil. Daring young men sometimes gamble on the pavement in the night, having set a guard at the corner to whistle when a policeman is approaching. But mostly they just group about and chat with the prostitutes. Before the war you could have got one for a dollar or even two shillings, but since the Americans came the girls sharpened themselves up and wouldn't be had for less than five Yankee dollars. Young girls from the country districts augmented the ranks, and there was keen rivalry. But a lot of men had girls who did that sort of thing and brought back the money for them, and they lived without working.

Joe Martin was born in George Street. Joe might easily have not been born. It was long before the war. Business was fairly prosperous in Trinidad, you could get a tin of condensed milk for six cents, sleep with a woman for a shilling, and go to a double feature at the cinema for a penny. The girl who bore him had many boy friends: "Dey go do for she," the neighbours warned, but Ethel paid them no mind. At an early age she found out that whoring was the easiest way to make a living.

Her aunt, known to one and all as Ma Lambie, was one of those people who form part of a community. If you probed into her past she became a mystery. But taken for granted, she was just an ugly, frowning Negress with great bowed legs—it seemed her legs bowed because the upper part of her body was just huge breasts, like buffers. She always wore a coloured piece of cloth on her head, "to stop de dew from falling on me."

Ma Lambie, as she made accra and float, told Ethel that if she went on like that she would only turn out to be a worthless whore, but Ethel asked her what the hell she was before her breasts got flabby and her skin wrinkled.

When Joe began, Ethel rushed to Ma Lambie to seek advice about an abortion. What she said was, "Oh gawd, aunty, yuh go help me trow away dis chile?"

Ma Lambie looked back on her own barren years and pondered the situation. She was getting old, a child ought to comfort her. She cursed Ethel roundly for fifteen minutes, and when the girl was crying and bawling oh gawd and wringing her hands, she stopped abruptly and asked, "Who is de fadder?"

Ethel's tears and moans ceased immediately and she said hopelessly, "Ah don't even know for sure. Ah was with John Monday night, and a soldier Tuesday night, and den Ah was walking in Frederick Street, looking at pretty tings in de glasscase—"

Joe Martin came. He lived under the bulky, grotesque shadow of Ma Lambie, and he never knew his mother and they never knew his father. Ma Lambie used to beat Joe every day. She clouted him behind the head if a stick wasn't near or gave him a jolt with her elbow as he hung on to her skirt while she was making souse in the kitchen.

As he grew up, the stick grew in proportion. She would say, when she struck him and the stick bounced off his hardened skin, "A-a, yuh getting man now, Ah have to get something else to beat yuh wid now."

By the time she was using a heavy piece of mangrove wood —what she used as fuel—Joe was sixteen years old, but his mind was much older, and his body was tough with hard work and blows.

The last time Ma Lambie beat Joe was a Saturday morning. He remembered it well, thinking back on his life when he was a man.

The barrackyard was buzzing with female life. Men who had no work lounged about on the steps or under trees, watching their women work. Some were playing cards, sitting in a circle under a mango tree, and a group of boys were intent on the production of a steel band instrument from a rubbish can they had stolen from the roadside the night before. The women were washing or cooking or sewing. The smell of the various ingredients which they put in black pudding was strong in the air. Little naked children screamed and jumped about, playing in the earth with stones, scraps of wood, bits of paper, anything they could lay their hands on. Those not old enough crawled and encountered the delight of a stump, a yellow leaf, or a broken bottle.

Ma Lambie was calling Joe. Cognizant of the power in her voice, she was sure Joe was nowhere in the yard. Once he had been hiding under the mango tree, watching the older boys and men play wapee, a gambling game with cards, and when she called he hadn't answered. But that only happened once. It could never happen again. Blows, blows, blows. After that beating she was sure if Joe was crippled he would drag his body a mile if she called.

"Joe! Joe!" she screamed, and her voice and fierce demeanour struck terror in the little children and they stopped playing and ran out of her path.

"Joe! Is way dat blasted boy gone to at all?" She came to the bank of the Dry River. She looked under the bridge and she saw him, with four other boys.

"Joe!" she screamed again, but rage choked her voice and it didn't carry. She brandished the mangrove wood in the air like a warrior about to do battle. "Wait till Ah catch yuh, oh God, yuh little black nigger!"

The boys were gathered around a dog they had dragged out of the water. It must have been dead for days, lying in the drain until rain fell and the water washed it down to a bend in the canal where it had lodged fast against debris. The boys had challenged each other to pull it out, and Joe had poked a bamboo and pushed the bloated, rotting body on the bank.

Now they stood around the carcass.

"Look at 'e eye," Joe said. "It look like 'e dead long time. An' fuss 'e stink!"

"Is a good ting if we cud get it by de school an' frighten dem girls wid it!"

No one saw Ma Lambie as she crept up, her hands behind her back so that the mangrove lay along her spine, out of sight. She stood off a little way, and her face assumed a change. She swallowed three times before the rage went into her belly. And she worked her face until the tightness there went. She even parted her thick lips and tried to smile.

"Joe, dou-dou darling boy, I was calling yuh so long, yuh didn't hear yuh aunty?" Her voice was wheedling.

The boys looked up. Joe stared at his grandmother with fear. Then, as if the tone of her voice had just registered, he opened his mouth in amazement. He sniffed the air suspiciously, like an animal. He was crouched on the ground, and the bigness of Ma Lambie was like a force keeping him down. He wanted to get up but she held him there with her eyes.

She was speaking, still in that amazing manner. "Dou-dou, is cuckoo dat Ah just cook, Ah bring some for you, love. Come nar, look Ah have it hide behind me back."

The other boys tried to get behind her to see if she was speaking the truth. But Ma Lambie backed away.

"Don't go, Joe, she go beat yuh!"

"She lie, Joe, she ain't have no cuckoo!"

"Don't mind dem, dou-dou"—she put honey in her voice—"yuh don't believe yuh old grandma?"

"Is true grandma? Is true?" he faltered, playing for time.

"Come an' see, sugar-pie, come, dou-dou."

Joe approached warily, his hands tensed and raised to ward off the blows. And when he was near enough, Ma Lambie's rage came back from her belly to her throat, and her eyes gleamed. The mangrove stick descended on Joe's back with all the force of her two arms. She screamed, "Oh God, yuh nasty nigger, Ah go kill yuh wid blows today! Yuh ent hear me calling yuh?"

Joe fell to his knees, cringing and writhing like a snake, but he didn't cry. Three times the stick descended, and Ma Lambie's voice grew hoarse.

The fourth time the stick cleaved empty air and struck the concrete. It split as if with an axe. Joe had slid away, pushing his bleeding body as if he were sinking his heels in the hard concrete.

Ma Lambie breathed deep with her exertions. Her great breasts rose and fell, and she trembled and perspiration ran down her face. She looked around at the other boys. "Allyuh ent shame! Is by dead dog allyuh go play?"

"And wat happen for dat?" one of them shouted, angry because his friend had been beaten. "Yuh can't do we anyting. Yuh must be take we for Joe! Joe too damn stupid. He big and strong, and he does still let an old woman like you beat him. If I was he Ah tumble you all over de place!"

They spoke about it for weeks after—and Ma Lambie was afraid to show her face in public; she locked herself in her room and wouldn't come out—how Joe, as if the devil had got into him, got slowly to his feet, gasping, and bending his arms to and fro as if measuring his strength; how his eyes had turned red, and how he had taken up the piece of bamboo and advanced slowly on Ma Lambie, who was so shocked she couldn't say a word. For weeks afterwards, in the barrackyard, in George Street and near the market, in the shops and on the pavements, it was a delicious scandal, a big "bacchanal."

"But neighbour, yuh hear how Ma Lambie grandson well beat she up? Yes, man, down in de Dry River, de tables turn. I hear he beat she, and beat she, and everybody say how it good for she, and nobody won't stop Joe. He follow she home, pelting wild cuff in she back and in she head. It was de sweetest fite for ah long time. Ah hear now she too fraid him."

Two things happened. Joe suddenly became a man, capable of loving and hating deeply. He decided to leave the school he attended in Nelson Street—parallel to George Street—and find a job. And Ma Lambie became a cringing, frightened old woman. Sometimes in the kitchen she talked to herself, cursing and abusing the world for taking advantage of a woman in her old age, waving her hands as if she were mad. But whenever Joe was around she kept quiet, looking at him out of the corners of her eyes. When he came home from gambling or idling about the city, she had an enamel cup of tea hot on the table, and a large slice of bake and fried saltfish all ready for him.

Joe didn't bother with her. He just kept to himself, silent, thinking a little about the future. He never had cause to strike Ma Lambie again.

One Saturday night he was supporting a lamp post at the corner of Queen and George Streets, listening to a wayside preacher.

Clad in a white flowing gown, a string of black beads hanging round his neck and a Bible in his hand, the bearded preacher walked up and down the pavement, sometimes shaking the book, sometimes lifting his eyes to the stars and spreading out his hands, beseeching mercy for the sinning people. A sickly bottle flambeau lighted the scene. Three women, dressed in gaudy silk robes, accompanied the preacher. They stood up near the wall and sang "Onward Christian Soldiers" and "Abide with Me." The light from the flambeau cast their shadows high on the wall. A sheet of newspaper was spread on the pavement and occasionally a penny or a cent was dropped on it. It was an unwritten law that any barrack folk giving more than a penny would be ostracized for showing off on the others.

If Ma Lambie was ill she still came to the meetings to sing and pray, her neck wrapped in cotton flannel. Nothing in the world could stop her. All her sins were washed away on Saturday night. When she prayed, she didn't pray for anything, she prayed for everything. She mumbled prayers for the whole sinning world. She shut her eyes tight and moved her lips, and the clean waters washed her soul. But she never remembered her prayers.

Joe watched and listened at the meeting. He saw his grandmother lapping up the words of the preacher like she was hungry, rolling her eyes and her tongue wetting her lips. And she sang all the hymns. She opened her mouth wide and sang the loudest. She sang with such fervour that the neighbours whispered among themselves sympathetically, "De spirit of de Lord possess she, sure."

The preacher bellowed, "There will be weeping and wailing and gnashing of teeth!"

The singers said, "Yes! Yes!" And Ma Lambie screamed, "Oh God, listen to the word, ye sinners! Wash yuh sins away!"

Joe wasn't paying any particular attention, because Ma Lambie used to drag him along every Saturday night, and he knew the whole proceedings by heart. He turned to a man at his side and said, "John, Ah want ah job, man."

John, a notorious gambler, laughed loudly. "But hear he! It have so much work down in de Yankee bases, men reaping harvest for so, and yuh say yuh want work! Dey paying good money down Chaguaramas, man, why yuh don't go?"

Joe went, the next Monday. He got a job easily, but it was a lot of hard work, preparing the swampy land for the buildings the Americans were putting up. Trucks used to take the men to work from the city, and he had to get up early to be on time. When he began to work Ma Lambie took to washing his clothes and keeping the tea hot by the coal-pot, but Joe never used to tell her anything at all. The first day he got paid she made a special supper of black pudding and souse, and she bought a bottle of rum from her own money and put it on the table and waited for him.

But Joe didn't come home until it was after midnight. And he was drunk. She asked him for some money, and he told her flatly to go to hell, that as soon as he had enough saved he was going to clear out and she would never see him again.

Joe gave his money to Rita to keep for him. Rita lived next door, and when Ma Lambie got to find out she abused the girl so much that finally she had to move and go to live with an aunt in Nelson Street.

Joe never courted Rita or anything like that. It was just sort of decided between them that when they had enough money—Rita worked as a housemaid with a rich white family in St. Clair, a beautiful residential district—they would go away and live together. When they talked about it they quarrelled, because Rita wanted to go in the country to live and Joe didn't want to leave the Dry River area. He was a member of the best steel band in that part of the city, and that was enough reason —he couldn't leave the boys. But Rita insisted, and as time went by Joe speculated on what an entirely different life would be like, to live in a clean house and eat good food. He didn't have many friends, he had grown up silent, learning from what he saw and heard and felt. The most noise Joe made was when he was playing the tenor kettle in the steel band.

When Ma Lambie realized Joe was serious she began to get sudden attacks and pains all over her body, wailing about old age and moaning in the night how she had worked herself to the bone to send Joe to school and bring him up, and now he was going to desert her. "Oh gawd oh, wat Ah go? Ah don't even know if yuh poor modder alive, is two years since Ah see she last."

But Joe ignored her, and once more her attitude became aggressive and bullying. Fancying herself safe because Joe refused to talk or have anything to do with her, she struck him as much as she could with her tongue. "Yuh little black bitch, dat is all de gratitude yuh have. Yuh tink yuh is big shot because yuh working for plenty Yankee money. But dat same woman Rita go do for yuh! Go on giving she all yuh money! Yuh go find out one day wen de mark bust, she go leave yuh and go whoring all over de place—every gul who born in George Street does turn whore!" If Joe made a sudden movement she would run behind the door and, drawing it against her body, continue her abuse from there.

But no matter what she told Joe she couldn't draw a word from him, because he knew he would never forget all the hate and blows and hunger he had lived through. When she stopped washing his clothes he took his laundry to Rita. When she refused to leave food for him or to prepare any for him to take to work, he bought sandwiches in a Chinaman's parlour in Queen Street. Sometimes he went round by Rita in the night and said, "Girl, Ah hungry." And Rita made black soup with dumplings and vegetables, to show him at the same time she could cook his favourite food as good or better than Ma Lambie.

"Joe," she said one night as they strolled around the Queen's Park Savannah, "Ah hear plenty houses for rent up Barataria."

"Is which part dat is?" Joe asked.

"Well, Ah never hear dat! Yuh mean a born Trinidadian like you don't know which part Barataria is? Boy, is just bout four miles from here, on the Eastern Main Road. It near to Caledonia, man, where Buttards living. Plenty taxis and bus, so yuh cud come to work on time."

"Dat good," he said noncommittally.

"But Ah telling yuh," Rita urged, "we cud live dere. We have bout one hundred dollar save up, we could coast on dat. Joe, Ah getting tired waiting, man."

They sat down on a bench and Joe said, "Well, if yuh tired yuh know wat to do."

"Yuh see how yuh always picking quarrel? Is not so Ah mean it. But de sooner de better, yuh don't tink?"

Joe nodded. He was thinking about all the fetes in Port of Spain he would miss. But anyway he could always spend a night or so with the boys. He didn't have to stick to Rita's tail just because they were going to live together. Buttards was always in town even though he was living in Caledonia.

The next week they got a house to rent in Barataria, paying an agent fifty dollars' reward. They moved up without telling a soul. Ma Lambie broadcast the news in the neighbourhood, calling down curses on the youth of today, and it was the subject of conversation for a week before people began to forget.

Tiger's neighbours were the Martins. They lived in a yellow and brown house built of concrete bricks, with glass windows. They had running water and a septic tank. They used an electric stove in the kitchen.

Joe Martin couldn't appreciate the amenities his money and home offered. He threw cigarette butts on the floor, wore his clothes dirty, and cursed when Rita rebuked him.

"Is so we black people can't get on," she would storm. "Yuh keeping de house dirty like ah pig. Yuh won't even go in de yard an' clean it wen yuh doing nutting on ah Sunday morning. Yuh drinking yuh rum and yuh cursing so much dat even

de chile start to cuss now. De oder day Ah sending him by
Tall Boy shop for ah tin of milk, he tell me go for de damn ting
meself. Is only wen Ah blade some licks in 'im dat 'e went."

The child was Rita's sister's boy, Henry. Rita was keeping him
because her sister had gone to Venezuela with a man. Joe had
objected strongly, but when he heard that the boy's mother
would send money to keep him, he shrugged and said he would
have nothing to do with it. Henry began to call Joe and Rita Pa
and Ma from the first day. They were growing to love him,
because Rita couldn't have any children of her own.

Henry listened wide-eyed when they quarrelled. The clash
of words, the gesticulations, got him excited. One night
Joe hurled a bottle at Rita, and Henry went running across
the track by the hibiscus fence. "Mr. Tiger, Mr. Tiger," he
screamed, "hide me! Ma and Pa fighting!"

During the day Rita would stand by the fence and gossip
to Urmilla as she swept the mango leaves from the yard. "Ah
never see ah man so in me born days," she said, "ah fuss he bad!
He like to drink rum too bad. Why we creole can't live like
Indian, quiet and nice?"

Urmilla was embarrassed. She knew from experience that
Indians fought and quarrelled just as much. Didn't she have a
mark on her shoulder where an empty tin had struck her when
her own father and mother were fighting? It was the same
thing all over. Only white people. If they could only be like
white people!

When the mango season was coming in—the tree in Tiger's
yard had begun to flower—Urmilla went to Rita one morning.
She was washing clothes in a tub; she bent backwards and forwards like a piece of machinery, scrubbing the dirt out of Joe's
clothes and grumbling to herself. Her black face glistened,
perspiration ran in little streams down the back of her neck.

Urmilla whispered in her ear. Rita passed a suddy hand across her forehead and straightened the flowered cloth on her head.

"Well, yuh don't know wat it is? Yuh in baby, girl!"

"Wat dat mean, Ma?" Henry asked.

"Get yuh little tail from here and get dress for school," Rita snapped and slapped Henry on his buttocks with her soapy hand. Suds flew, and Henry ran inside.

"Yes, girl"—her voice softened as she turned back to her neighbour—"yuh is going to have ah baby."

And she related about the time when her sister was having Henry, how she didn't have to go to any doctor. "Not even ah midwife was dere," she said, "is me who deliver de baby for she. It was easy for she, but Ah don't know bout you," and she appraised Urmilla's frail frame. "Yuh better eat plenty food and get strong," she advised.

Tiger came in from the garden when the sun sank. He had carried the cow with him because there was good grazing grass near his land, and he could keep an eye on the animal. Now it preceded him, trailing a rope, stopping to crunch at a crop of grass on the roadside. He had gone in to Tall Boy's shop for a shot of rum. He did that every evening now, when he was going back home. He never drank too much—just enough to make him feel big.

He tied the cow under the mango tree. "Ohe, Urmilla," he called.

The girl came out. "Tiger!" she said excitedly, "something happen!"

"What?" he asked, trying to show a calmness he didn't feel.

"I going to have the baby!"

"Is true? Who tell you? How you know? Is a boy chile?" A new path opened in the jungle of his mind. He thought, Things happen so quickly.

"How I will know if is boy chile? Is Rita who tell me. She know all about those things."

The rum was warm in his belly. He did not know what was the right thing to say. But he was happy. He laughed. "Well, girl, I hope is a boy chile."

"You glad, Tiger, you glad?" she asked eagerly, and waited for his answer before breathing.

"I have to think about these things," he said warily, "but is a good thing what happen."

When they went inside he said, "I open up account with Tall Boy this evening. So you could trust things, and we will pay every week."

Later he sat on the floor, sharpening his hoe with a stone. She asked, "How the garden coming?"

"Is a lot of work, girl. That land look rich, but I have to do plenty weeding before I fork it. It look like they have a swamp down there. Plenty other people have garden. Lettuce taking good, and water cress. But ochro and melongene would take too."

He got up after testing the sharpness of the hoe with his thumbnail. He went to the cupboard he had made from a soapbox.

"Is about one hundred dollar remain," he said, counting the bills slowly. "We have to careful. The garden have plenty work yet before we start to plant. You better start selling milk from the cow."

Tiger knew that money was necessary, that life could be hard, roti-less without it. He had seen his father and mother scrape together the remains of supper for breakfast in the morning, and how often had he gone out in the cane with nothing but a weak cup of tea in his belly? Hours and hours in the blazing sun. Out there in the sun one forgot hunger in the swing of cutlass on fat, juicy stalks of cane. There was no time to think—it was work, work until the back ached, and the days burned into weeks and months.

But if there was any way of getting by without money, he would take it. He preferred ten pounds of rice to a dollar bill: he couldn't eat the dollar. And if he had his way he would trade his crops in Tall Boy's shop for flour and cooking oil and perform all negotiations by an exchange of the things he possessed for the things he wanted. So he thought as he lay on the floor that night. There were so many things he did not understand, so many bees in the hive of his brain. He figured this was so because he had very little to offer in exchange. And he thought that when he planted his crops, and reaped his harvest of ochro, melongene, and bodee, he would have plenty to offer in exchange for all the things he wanted to discover, uncover. He didn't know whom he would make this bargain with, but didn't he find out where the estate office was when he wanted to rent the land?

Then he thought of the baby in Urmilla's belly. He put out his hand fearfully and touched her where it was. Urmilla stirred. He drew back his hand. For a long time he watched with wonder. And then a serious thought came. He began to pray fervently in the night, Oh God, let it be a boy chile.

When he milked the cow in the morning Urmilla said mischievously, "Let we put water in it. It go get more."

"It have no reason for that," Tiger reproved. "My father say not to do anybody anything until they do you. We new in this place; let we live good with everybody."

"I was only making a joke, yes," Urmilla said. "And too besides, plenty trouble in that. One time Sookdeen did put water in he milk, and the police get to find out. He get charge fifty dollar in court. Weself used to buy from him. Ma say how he is a thief, and since that time she stop him tying the cow in we land to graze."

She was fanning away smoke from the fire. Tiger said, "You know what? You better cook some food for me to carry in the garden. From now, I go work whole day. Everything go finish quicker."

"All right. I go go with you and sell the milk."

She had never sold anything before, but she wasn't embarrassed to walk around the streets with the pail on her head, shouting, "Aaye! Milk! Fresh cow milk!"

One woman told her, "Allyuh Indian too wutless! Allyuh does sell water flavour wid milk!"

"Oh no, madam," Urmilla said quickly, "just this morning I make a joke and tell my husband to put water, and he get so vex."

"Dat young man Ah does see passing wid de cow and de hoe, he is yuh husband?"

"Yes."

"But how allyuh Indian people does married so young! He still look like ah little boy, and poor you, yuh still have yuh modder features."

Womanhood squeezed out of the earth of Urmilla. "I only look small," she said proudly, tossing her long hair on her shoulders as she threw her head back, "but I going to have a baby, though!"

The woman looked shocked. "*Eh bien!*" she exclaimed and shook her head sadly. "All rite, me chile, Ah go take milk. Yuh cud bring ah pint every day. Yuh know de schedule price is eight cents?"

She was lucky. At the eleventh house she sold the last pint and went home in triumph.

Rita asked, "Way yuh been to, girl?"

"Girl, I selling milk now. I make regular customers already."

"But a-a, is so yuh does do ting? Yuh don't know dat I wud buy from yuh meself? Yuh must leave ah bottle for me every morning, man."

And they went on to talk of Joe and Tiger. Always Rita complained of Joe. "Don't let yuh husband get like dat, chile," she warned the Indian girl, "because life go be hell."

CHAPTER THREE

Mango season came. In the Northern Range the trees were in full fruit, and schoolchildren on holiday roamed the hills all day long, stealing in the gardens, hurling stones at those they couldn't reach, eating the green ones with pepper and salt. The markets were glutted with the fruit—mango *veh*, mango cutlass, mango *do-dous*, mango leatherskin, mango bread, mango turpentine, mango cheese. The schoolchildren sang:

> "Mango long is to make it strong!
> Mango rose is to lift up she clothes!"

One Saturday morning Henry looked at the rose mango tree in Tiger's yard. Ripe ones had fallen on the ground, but he didn't want those. He wanted fresh ones. He thought of climbing the tree silently and stealing a few, but the risk was too great: either Rita or Miss Tiger was sure to see him.

"Good morning, Miss Tiger!"

"Who is that, Henry? What you want, boy?"

"Miss Tiger, please tanks for some mango. Ma say please to give she some."

"How you going pick them? The rod too heavy for you." She looked at the long bamboo rod Tiger had brought home from the bush.

"Oh, Ah cud climb," he said quickly. And without waiting for an answer he clambered up and perched himself between a fork and began to eat, dropping the skin on the roof of the hut.

"Throw down some green one for me," Urmilla called, shading her eyes with her hands from the glare of the sun as she looked up. "I think I go begin to make *achar* and sell."

The rose mangoes grew red, juicy, and the tree was laden. Urmilla too had grown stronger. Her cheeks were rosy, her breasts high and pointed. All these things Tiger noted with satisfaction.

I only hope is a boy chile, he prayed in the night, in Tall Boy's shop, in the field as he bent his back to the soil. He would have threatened Urmilla and commanded her to bear a boy, but Joe Martin had told him that that wouldn't help. "Wat is to is, must is," Joe said.

But Urmilla felt it was her bounden duty to bring forth a boy. Night and day she prayed, Oh God, help me to please Tiger, put a boy chile in my belly.

One day when a high wind was dropping mangoes in the yard she felt a movement in her stomach and she told Rita. Rita consulted an almanac and nodded her head.

"If tings go rite, shud be some time next week," she said.

Tiger was growing impatient. Every night he asked her, "What about this boy chile? When it coming?"

And Urmilla said, "You can't force nature, Tiger. Same way with your cabbage and melongene, same way with me."

The next week, for the first time, Rita went into the hut to look around. She burst into instant abuse. "Is how dat man expect yuh to have yuh baby on de floor? Is ah damn shame. Allyuh ain't have ah bed?"

"Not yet, man. Later we going to buy one, though."

Rita went back without answering and dismounted the bed

on which she and Joe slept. Piece by piece she brought it over, cursing Tiger. She mounted the bed in a corner of the hut.

"Stop doing hard work," she ordered. "Yuh must lay down on dis bed. And don't let dat damn Tiger sleep on it. Put 'im on de floor, near to yuh. And if yuh feeling any pains, call me. I go deliver dat baby for yuh, girl, don't fraid."

"But man, Rita, what Joe go say when he come home and ain't see the bed? Suppose he beat you? You not fraid?"

"You don't worry wid dat, nar. Is my own just as much as he own wen it come to dat."

"You too good. I don't know what to tell you."

Joe Martin came home and "Wat de hell happen to de bed?"

"Keep yuh big mouth shut. Yuh neighbour have it. She going to have ah baby."

"So wat de arse we have to do wid dat? Dem Indian people does have plenty money hide away. Why Tiger don't buy ah bed for he wife?"

"It ent have time for dat—suppose she make de baby tonight? Is true tings ain't so rosy wid we dese days, but still. And too besides, shame on yuh! Yuh grudging poor people yuh bed! Is yuh neighbour! How much time yuh ain't get tings from dem for nutting?"

"To arse wid all ah dat! Dis is damn slackness! And who is you? Yuh playing midwife? Suppose someting go wrong? Who de arse tell yuh to interfere in de coolie people business?"

Tiger said, "We can't allow this thing to happen." But he was afraid to carry back the bed. Suppose the baby came in the night? He felt he had failed in not getting a bed already, but both of them were accustomed to sleeping on bags on the floor. He didn't know what to do.

Urmilla sat on the bed. "Boy, it have spring, feel how soft it is! You ever sleep on a bed before? My father and mother had one, but I used to sleep on the floor. But they really good to we, and look how they is creole and we is Indian! But, Tiger, suppose it not boy chile?"

"It better be boy chile, I warning you."

"But, Tiger man, I can't help if God put a girl!"

"Well, he better put a boy, you hear."

"Girl chile good too, you know, don't mind what people say. I use to cut cane just as good as my brother and them."

"I telling you, I don't want no girl chile. Too besides, you talking too much. You should sleep and take plenty rest."

But nothing happened that night, though he sat up and looked at her for a long time, until he fell asleep with his head resting against the bed.

The next night it happened. He rushed over to Joe's house and pounded the door. "Rita! Joe! Come quick! The thing happening!"

Rita came out with her slippers flying and a dress halfway on.

"Ah want plenty hot water," she snapped at Tiger and ran into the hut.

Tiger put the water on the fire with shaky hands. Joe came up and stood watching him. "Well, yuh not even offering me ah drink?"

"No rum in the house, man," he said, bending down and blowing the fire. And again he felt ashamed; he should have had rum in the house.

"So wat happen? It ain't too late to wake up Tall Boy. Ain't yuh open account wid him? I could tell 'im yuh say to send ah bottle. De shop ain't far from here. Yuh shud have ah bottle to celebrate, man."

"Well go then, just tell him I send you, and he will give you." Tiger pushed more wood in the fire and kept lifting the lid off the pot, as if he expected the water to be boiling in a minute.

By the time Joe returned it was boiling, and Tiger poured it into a basin and carried it inside, tiptoeing.

"Put it down and get to hell out," Rita called over her shoulder.

He went out sheepishly. He couldn't show her he was a man when he didn't know what it was all about.

He sat down on the back steps with Joe and took a drink. He said, "Joe, you was there when Rita sister was having Henry? What happen?"

"Oh, nutting at all. It ent have nutting in dat, people does have baby every day. De time wen Rita sister did having Henry, I and he fadder was chopping liquor for so, we drink two bottle, and we play cards until two o'clock in de morning."

"I feel as if I shouldn't drink. This is a big thing for me, Joe."

A sharp cry came from the hut, and Tiger sprang to his feet. Joe laughed. "Don't get excited, yuh ain't hear nutting yet. Have ah drink and cool down."

Tiger drank a tall one and felt better. "I sorry we have to borrow the bed, Joe. As soon as I get fix up I going to buy one."

"Yuh better buy ah crib instead, or ah hammock for de baby. So wat yuh doing? Yuh going and have big christening party, plenty food and drink? Big Indian fete? Ah know how allyuh Indian people like allyuh roti and rum, you know."

"I ain't decide nothing yet, man. Pundit have to give him name, under what star he born."

"Wat about de family down Chaguanas? Yuh ain't sending message to tell dem?"

"Well, look at that! I nearly forget about that, yes. Joe, you could write?"

Joe shook his head. "I cud live without writing," he said.

"You mean big man like you can't write?"

"Wat happen for dat? Yuh talking, you cud write?"

"No, but I mean, I smaller than you. And too besides, you come from Port of Spain, and I from the country." But he was glad Joe couldn't write, because Joe was a man.

"Dey have plenty people who can't write," Joe said, "and dey living happy."

"Well, I know what I go do. We go have to go San Juan to see the Pundit. When he give me name for the boy, I go ask him to write my family and tell them."

It was about ten o'clock. A wind blew and shook the mango tree; a fruit fell with a thud in the yard. Joe took it up and washed it with a calabash of water from the barrel. He sucked the mango. A half-moon softened the darkness. Radios had gone off one by one, until it was very quiet, except for the occasional barking of dogs.

"Wat yuh tinking about? Come fire ah drink, man."

"I just studying about when the boy chile come."

"Well, sit down quiet, nar. Keep yuh tail quiet, it ain't have long again. Rita always putting sheself in oder people business."

Rita came out, wiping her hands in a towel. "Everyting all rite, yuh wife have strength, she more able dan Ah did tink."

"Where the baby?" Tiger asked, shaking all over, as if he had ague.

"It inside nar, but wait a little bit, Ah ent finish wid Urmilla yet."

"Is a pretty boy? He resemble me?"

"Who de hell tell yuh is ah boy? Dat is all allyuh Indian people want, boy chile, boy chile, as if woman is ah sin! Well, is ah girl, if yuh want to know."

Tiger left them and walked off into the night, his head reeling. So many things exploded like a sandbox seed in his mind, shocking him, pitching him about because he did not know. He felt robbed. Maybe there was something he could have done to make sure a boy would be born—maybe there was some medicine Urmilla could have taken that Rita didn't know anything about. Or maybe he hadn't prayed hard enough. He remembered the time when a white minister used to come from San Fernando and preach in Chaguanas. Once his mother had asked the minister, "If I want something plenty, and I ask God, he would give me?" The minister replied, "Ask and it will be given unto you." Tiger didn't know what it was his mother wanted, but she never got it. She went back to the man and said, "Sahib, I pray hard, but nothing come." And the minister said, "God knows best, perhaps it is better that way."

Now he thought what was the use of praying if God already knew what to do?

He walked across the land and sat down on a bank overlooking his garden. When he was in Chaguanas he was never worried by his thoughts. Was worry one of the signs of a man? And all the incidents since his marriage came like giant hands out of the night to hold him down. The sudden movement from boyhood to manhood, his hut, his acquiring the land to plant a garden, the nights with Urmilla, days turning the soil, the baby just born. The hands clutched at his throat. He wanted to cry out in terror and run until he couldn't run again. He threw himself down on the ground and his fingers clutched tufts of grass and pulled them out. He shut his eyes tightly; night came into his head. And then it seemed as if the hands were relaxing their hold on him. The grip on his heart slackened. Waves rocked him gently. Suddenly he was aware of being all alone in the bush; even night insects were still, and the trees were motionless. He backed away on the grass and shut his eyes again.

Suddenly he sprang up. He was not alone. He had a wife. He had a child. He put the picture of them in front of his mind to ward off all the things he didn't know, which came to choke him from the dark. He said aloud, "I not alone. I have a wife and a chile. Don't mind it not boy chile. I is a man."

And a man should be home with his wife and child. Perhaps something had happened to Urmilla. Perhaps she had died while he was walking in the bush.

With a cry like a wounded deer he darted through the bush.

Tiger never completely reconciled himself to the fact that the child was a girl—even after the Pundit in San Juan said it would be lucky. "Call she Chandra," the Pundit instructed, consulting a book. He promised to write to Chaguanas.

Tiger wasn't going to hold any feast to celebrate. When their relatives came they didn't bring any expensive gifts. Just a few toys that had no lasting value. One was a miniature piano, and Urmilla was fascinated with it. When she was a child she never had any toys. She struck the notes and her eyes grew bright.

Tiger's *bap* seemed to take it that the marriage had turned him into a man right away. He adopted a man-to-man attitude with Tiger, and Tiger tried to keep up with him. His father asked, "How everything going? Yuh gettam land to buy? Have garden? Good crop?"

It was just like the wedding ceremony, only not as exciting. Maybe because he was getting to be a man.

Six of them came, crowding into the hut and laughing and talking, and everyone said how the baby resembled Tiger. The women whispered in the corner to Urmilla and she blushed and laughed. She held the baby proudly in her arms, and Tiger thought that she was learning to be a woman too.

He wanted to offer his father a drink, but it was a struggle between his desire to show he was growing up and a fear of being rebuked. But he thought that the baby was born, and they should have a drink or two. He said half boldly, "*Bap*, I could get some rum in the shop. I have account there now, you know. You would care to have a little drink?"

The old man said, "Well, you should haveam here already! After all, you is man now, boy, and you must haveam drink in house for when friend come."

Tiger thought, To my wife, I man when I sleep with she. To *bap*, I man if I drink rum. But to me, I no man yet.

He met Joe in the shop and Joe said, "A-a, Tiger, Ah ain't see yuh to talk to since de night yuh out off wen de baby born. Come and fire one, man."

They had one and Tiger invited Joe to meet his parents. Joe said, "Wat yuh have? Curry chicken? Roti? Plenty rum?"

"Is just a little thing, man," Tiger said, "nothing much. The family come, and we having a few drinks. Come and go, man. You is my neighbour."

"Ah don't like dis business wid coolie people, nar. As is a freeness Ah will come."

After the first drink in the hut *bap* said, "Joe, I hear how you helpam *betah* when baby come. Is a good thing."

It was only the rum kept Joe in the hut. He shrugged his shoulders. "Me ain't do nutting—is de wife who help dem out. We is neighbours, yuh see." He felt uncomfortable.

But Tiger didn't notice. The rum was making him giddy, he felt twice his size. He looked out the window and called out, "Rita! Come over, neighbour, and meet we family—and bring some more glass!"

The elders frowned and Urmilla's mother pulled her sari over her head in a significant movement.

Rita brought Henry with her. There was no formal introduction, she just waved her hand at them and gave Joe a nasty look out of habit. "Is how me dou-dou chile keeping, eh?" She took Chandra up and rocked her. "So Tiger buy ah hammock for she?"

While she spoke everyone listened and watched. An atmosphere of strain crept in; only Tiger and Urmilla seemed at ease. "Yes, we buy it when we went San Juan," Urmilla said. "She growing nice, you don't think so, Rita?"

"Is true! Is true! Is de fresh cow milk yuh does be drinking in de morning." She put the child back in the hammock and surveyed the room, confident of herself. She called for a drink. "Everybody must have ah drink together," she ordered.

Henry moved quietly to the hammock and when he was near enough put out his forefinger and touched the baby's cheek lightly. Urmilla's mother pinched him viciously on the arm. Henry began to cry. Rita did not see what happened. She drove him out. "Up to now yuh can't behave yuhself in people house," she snapped.

The boy went under the house and cried bitterly.

Tiger filled the glasses quickly and Rita passed them around. There was no refusing her. She forced the glasses into their hands. She poured most of Urmilla's drink in her own and said, like a mother, "Yuh not strong enough yet."

Urmilla smiled, and her mother pulled the sari on her head again.

Tiger said, "But, Rita, I think she could have a drink, man—"

Rita told him to keep his damn mouth shut, that she knew better than him. She turned to Joe. "Make a toast," she commanded.

Joe looked at her as if he wanted to kick her right there in front of everybody. But he said something about long life and health and swallowed his drink quickly.

Tiger saw a chance to prove he was getting to be a man. He

said, "I is the man of the house, and I have to answer Joe toast."

Urmilla moved with a sixth sense and filled the glasses again. Tiger looked at her and smiled and she knew she had done the right thing.

But when he began to talk he found it wasn't going to be as easy as he thought, even with the rum in his head. "Well," he began waveringly, "I—we—glad to have family and friends here today, especially as the baby born. Is true we not rich and we have only a small thing here, but still, is a good thing. So let we make a little merry for the baby. I should really begin different, I don't know what happen to me. I should say, 'Ladies and gentlemens,' and then make speech. But I cannot speechify very good. I would learn, though—" That was as far as he could go. He felt he would talk foolishness if he continued, and he gulped his drink.

He wanted everyone to make a speech, but all the elders shook their heads. And it became awkward, just standing and looking at one another, as if something had gone wrong. Rita suddenly sniffed and cried out, "Oh gawd oh! Ah forget de pot on de fire!" and she ran out.

And Joe said, "Well, one for de road. Ah peeling off now," and after the drink he waved his hand and departed.

Immediately a babble of voices broke out in the hut.

"Is only nigger friend you makeam since you come?" his *bap* asked. "Plenty Indian liveam dis side. Is true them is good neighbour, but you must look for Indian friend, like you and you wife. Indian must keep together."

"Is I who pinch him, that is why he cry," Urmilla's mother said. "Nigger boy put he black hand in my *betah* baby face! He too fast again!"

"But, *mai*, these people good to us; we is friends. I does get little things from she, and sometimes she does borrow little things from me. They is not bad people."

Tiger said, "If it wasn't for them, I—we—wouldn't know what to do."

"What you *bap* say is right thing, though," his uncle said. "Nigger people all right, but you must let creole keep they distance. You too young to know about these things, but I older than you. Allyuh better make Indian friend."

Urmilla tucked the baby away with clean flour bag sheets and stood rocking the hammock after they had gone. Tiger touched the baby's cheek. He took up the piano and played some notes. The baby took no notice, but Urmilla was delighted. "Play more, Tiger," she whispered. "I like to hear it."

He thought "more" meant "louder" and he struck the notes harder. "S-s-sh, the baby must get plenty sleep," she said softly. Her *mai* had given her much advice on how to keep the child. Shades of responsibility moved in her mind. From the time the baby had come, a new power had swept through her, like wind. She marvelled in it, moved her tongue in her mouth to see if she could taste the sweetness flowing through her. She moved her hands over her body and through her hair, and when she felt the baby at her side, she had thought, I is woman now, and the thought had made her fearful and joyful at the same time.

Tiger sat on the step and watched night coming. The big thought he had postponed came back. It had happened when his parents talked about Joe and Rita. At the time rum was in his head, but now it was all clear. Why I should only look for Indian friend? What wrong with Joe and Rita? Is true I used to play with Indian friend in the estate, but that ain't no reason why I must shut my heart to other people. Ain't a man is a man, don't mind if he skin not white, or if he hair curl?

He thought how burned cane thrash went spinning in the wind helplessly. He and Urmilla would have been like that if Joe and Rita hadn't helped.

He found decision difficult. He was even angry with himself, and he thought that if he was so stupid, how would he explain things to his children when they grew up and asked questions?

Urmilla came and sat down beside him. She too watched the dark and the stars in the sky. She guessed what her husband was thinking, and she would have liked to talk it over with him, but she knew that Indian women just kept the house and saw after the children and didn't worry their men. But she wanted it to be different with them, that they could talk and laugh together, and share worries. Would Tiger stop her from talking to Rita? If he did, she would have to obey. It would be lonely with no one to share gossip.

It was as if he drew power from the darkness, as if in the struggle itself there was understanding and truth, if he could only find them. He pulled Urmilla's hand to him. The girl was glad. She held on tightly.

He thought, This must be growing up. I must be really coming man now.

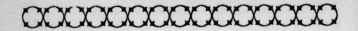

CHAPTER FOUR

The majority of Chinese in Trinidad are shopkeepers or launderers. Either one is prosperous business for them, and with typical Oriental attitude they stick to selling goods or washing clothes in preference to anything else. They began to trickle into the island in the latter half of the nineteenth century. Those who prospered sent for their families and encouraged others to come. They scattered all over the colony, in the villages and in the towns, in remote country districts and seaside resorts. The key to their success lay in hard work and the very little with which they could make themselves comfortable. Newcomers would work with an established shopkeeper for a number of years, then go into another district and open up their own shop or laundry.

In Trinidad there is a short-cut to identity. All Americans, for instance, are known as "Joes." East Indians are hailed as "Ram" or "Singh" or some other common name until an association is formed and introductions made. Though this method of identifying unknowns is not used among the middle or upper class, it is the custom of the working class to address strangers in this manner.

In the same way, all Chinese are "Chins." Not that it matters a great deal to the Chinaman, as long as his shop or laundry is well patronized. But if it happens that he takes unto himself a creole wife, she demands that he be addressed properly, in order to keep her own self-respect. However, there are some cases where by peculiarities or through their relationships with the people, Chinese shopkeepers have become possessors of names which they bear proudly, feeling themselves now truly accepted.

It was so in San Fernando, a thriving town forty miles south of Port of Spain, where Old Man became as one of the community. He had a large shop, and soon after he opened business he sent to China for help, and two countrymen came. Old Man used to sit on an empty saltfish barrel, clad in a dirty merino and a khaki pants, his wooden slippers so placed on the floor that he could slip into them at a moment's notice, and watch with satisfaction his assistants administering the business. Some customers, dissatisfied with the service they got, would refuse to buy any goods unless Old Man himself attended to them. After some time the aged Chinaman got accustomed to this flattery and used to stay behind the shop, coming to the front only on special business or when his presence was really necessary. But his life was ebbing away. He used to go to Mucurapo Street and smoke opium in a den behind a laundry every Saturday night. When the police raided the den Old Man had no place else to go to immediately. He died one night, coughing in his sleep. His assistants closed the shop for a day, and after that business went on as usual. But customers fell off after his death, and it was some time before the people in that part of the town got used to the assistants, though they never gave them any names.

In Barataria they began to call Tall Boy that from the very first, because he was tall and young. He had an almost Western face—his eyes didn't slant—and he spoke English in the same way as the working class, though he could read only a little.

Tall Boy had been working as an assistant in Port of Spain for some years and was well at home with Trinidadians, even adopting some local habits and manners of speech. He moved into Barataria with a pregnant wife and four little boys with scarcely a year between each of them. Mary was doomed to be always with child when she married Tall Boy, but she was Chinese and accepted it. When the women in the village got to know her well they said, "Is how dis Tall Boy running yuh down so? He must be full of blood!"

In a week he was settled, leaning over the counter and chatting familiarly with all who came into the shop. In the shops one does not ask for credit. It is "trust" me this or that until payday. In every shop there is a crumpled exercise book in which the names of debtors are kept, and an account of how much money they owe. Most business is done on this system, and Tall Boy did not delay for a moment in offering to trust the customers, though behind their backs he did make discreet inquiries as to whether they were honest.

Because most of the villagers came to buy their goods on a Saturday night, cluttering the shop and demanding attention at the same time, Tall Boy requested that they hand in lists of what they wanted by Friday, so he could have them ready the next day. He stayed up late—his home was just back of the shop, the same building—and made up the goods, putting the parcels in empty carton boxes. He kept the slips of paper on a piece of pointed wire hung on a nail for easy reference. But, despite this, every Saturday night the shop was crowded, and sometimes he had to shut the people in when it was time to close.

Tall Boy's children were part of the shop. Those who were old enough to go to school hid about the house until it was too late; Mary, filled with child, would go out in the road, her wooden slippers cloppety-clopping on the gravel, and call,

"Ling! Pewee! Achong!" and her voice went ringing in the neighbourhood. Then, when schooltime was past, the boys crawled from under the counter, behind the sacks of rice and sugar, the barrels of pork and saltfish. All day long they roamed the shop, tumbling the tins of milk Tall Boy lined neatly on the shelves, sitting on the counter and making ugly faces at the customers, getting in Tall Boy's way so much that sometimes he had to lift them in his arms or pass them on to a woman customer. If Mary came to assist him they held on to her skirt and followed her wherever she went. She and her husband petted the children extensively, yet with sudden anger would strike them, and when they burst out crying the customers would cry hush, hush, and play with their chubby cheeks.

Every morning other people's children passed the shop on their way to school, their slates and copybooks in satchels of coloured cloth, walking in that sweet wonder of childhood, standing here to watch a donkey cart pass, stumbling on a stone and looking at it with amazement, walking zigzag or backwards, in imitation of a driver, now on this side of the road, now on that, waiting impatiently for a small brother or sister who lingered and lagged, crying because it had to go to school.

Every morning, as they passed, they called out, "Pewee, come an' go to school!" But Pewee made them a "monkey face" and ran into the shop and hid behind the saltfish barrel. But when they had all gone, and no children came to the shop "for message," and they were tired playing among themselves, they used to wonder about school where all the other children were, and that part of the world around the grass-edged road. Soon they were being teased for not having trousers on. And when they clamoured for more clothes Mary knew it was high time she marched them off to school. She arranged with a neighbour for her children to take them as they passed the shop. The first morning she had them dressed, fidgeting in new trousers below their knees, and she locked them up in the house so they couldn't go in the shop. They went meekly enough, though Pewee hung back all the way, crying, and Ling had to hold his hand and drag him along.

In Trinidad one does not have to be a teacher or to be in possession of special qualifications to open up a kindergarten. All that is needed is a room in which to hold class, a blackboard, a few benches and desks. There were six of these kindergartens in Barataria, where the majority of people sent the children until they were old enough to attend the government school near the Eastern Main Road. It was a means of getting them out of the way for some time, so that domestic chores could be done in peace. Many middle-class people sent their children to these schools.

The school which Tall Boy's children attended was a popular one, it being in seventh street, about midway in the village. It was under a house, the dwelling itself being more than six feet above the ground, and the walls were nailed loosely together, so the children used to peep through the chinks to see who was passing outside when the teacher wasn't looking. The teacher was a Negro woman, a little past her youth but still going strong, entertaining American servicemen in the night to augment her earnings. She lived with her grandmother. Every morning she sat on the floor in front of her grandmother, who combed her hair. She was always going to iron her hair, to make it straight like white people or Indian people. In the gallery where they sat the sun would cast rays, and she would bask in the early warmth, feeling lazy to go and teach the children their abc, her great legs flat on the floor, her hands pressing down the front of her dress between her legs so nobody passing in the road could see anything. And the children, pushing the gate after passing over the plank of wood with which she had bridged the canal, would say, "Good morning, Miss!" just as she had trained them.

"Good morning! Good morning, children! John, wat yuh bring for teacher today, eh? Ah mango? Don't make too much noise in de yard, and don't get yuh clothes dirty. School will call just now."

Henry was the eldest boy in class. He was of age to attend the government school, but he dreaded it and screamed whenever Rita suggested it. He was also the most mischievous and disobedient. He never said "Miss" when he said "Good morning." Once the teacher asked him why, and he said, "My modder say is nough to say 'Good morning,' dat Ah ain't bound to say 'Miss' too." Having put away his book and slate, he set about drawing rude pictures of boys and girls on the wall in the back with chalk he had stolen from Miss. He had already beaten all the children, there was no one to fight. He could pitch marbles better than any of the boys; he encouraged them to wring buttons off their blouses and pants to play with.

The morning the Chinese children came to school he ganged up the rest against them. When it was recess—a midmorning break of ten or fifteen minutes—they gathered around the Chinese and sang:

> "Chinee, Chinee, never die,
> Flat nose and chinky eye!"

But Ling was no coward, even though Henry was bigger than he. He put his hands to his ears to shut out their voices and he sang:

> "Nigger is ah nation,
> Dey full of bodderation.
> Meet dem by de station,
> Dey stink wid perspiration!"

Then he turned to the Indians. "Everybody know allyuh does use ah bottle of water in de w.c. Ha ha!"

"Chinee does eat cat an' dog!"

"Nigger does smell stink wid perspiration!"

"Coolie people does eat wid dey hands!"

It became a general shouting fray. Everybody put their hands to their ears to express indifference to what the others said. A white-skinned girl, dressed neatly with a blue ribbon in her hair, was called, "Whitey cockroach!"

She retorted, "Black tar-baby!"

"Don't make so much noise!" Miss called from a window above. "Henry, Ah sure yuh start it. Just wait till Ah come down and cut ah switch from de hibiscus fence!"

After the first week Tall Boy's children refused to be taken by anybody—they wanted to go and come by themselves. Mary cautioned them to keep to the left side of the road and allowed them to have their own way, but just because they didn't have to, they went and came back with the other children. After another week it was one day in school and the next in the shop. Ling would say he had fallen and hurt his knee and couldn't walk, and Pewee and Achong refused to go without him. Only the threat of medicine could make them snatch their satchels, or if Tall Boy began to take off his belt in a threatening gesture.

It was not long before Tall Boy went to Port of Spain and obtained a licence from the police to sell spirituous liquors. He knew there could never be too many rumshops in the village. He extended the counter and opened a bar. It was successful from the first day. News of this latest item now being sold in the shop spread through the village, and men deserted their favourite bars to try out Tall Boy's. On two stools and soap boxes they sat. The bar became a place of rest and gossip and "firing one."

Tall Boy and Mary were busy from shop to bar. Especially on a Saturday night, labourers would come in from the fields and get together, and if things waxed warm they sang calypsoes and made a lot of noise after Tall Boy closed the shop; he had to coax them away or refuse to sell any more rum before they left.

On a Sunday the shop was closed, and Tall Boy pottered about the yard, mending his fowl coop or cooking a good Chinese lunch. But even on that day of rest housewives who had forgotten to buy salt or onions went around to the back of the shop and pounded loudly on the galvanized sheets nailed to the gate. Tall Boy would send one of the children to see who it was, though he knew he would have to go himself. "Look, Tall Boy, Ah forget to get salt, man. Reach ah pound for me, nar." Or somebody had run short of rum or wanted a bottle because friends had dropped in unexpectedly. So accustomed was he to these interruptions that he built a shelf at the back of the shop, and stored a quantity of goods, including a case of rum. "Put it in yuh pocket—don't let a policeman see yuh!" he cautioned, as he slipped the bottle wrapped in newspapers through a small opening in the gate. He usually made a little profit on Sundays by selling underweight or mixing water with the rum, but he felt justified in that he was taking a chance against the law, and besides, no one stood up to argue or check their parcels. But, on the whole, he treated his customers fairly and even generously at times, so that business was prospering and he was thinking of extending his premises.

Obliquely opposite to the shop, on a rich plot of land with a mango tree which the children stoned when it was in fruit, Otto, another Chinaman, had a parlour where he sold sweets, aerated drinks, bread and cakes. Otto had a baby face and a forehead which went back until it met closely cropped, straight black hair. Otto smoked opium in Port of Spain. He was listless and dull and attracted very little business, though his was the only well-stocked parlour in that part of Barataria, with enough room for him to have a few tables with chairs. The only thing Otto might have sold often was snowball. But Otto was too lazy to shave the ice. All day long he lay on a bed in an adjoining room with the door open. He ignored customers when he saw them with a glass or jug—he knew they wanted snowball—and rolled over, turning his back to the door and pretending to be fast asleep. Early every morning a boy from the bakery near San Juan delivered fresh bread and cakes. Otto put these in the front of the glass case, to make a good show, and sold the stale ones from the day before. Sometimes he shut the parlour and went into Port of Spain when the urge for opium was too strong, and when the boy came to deliver the cakes, or the truck brought ice from Port of Spain, there was no one to receive them. Otto eventually employed a small boy from the village to work in the parlour. The boy shaved ice furiously and for a week the snowball sale soared. He sold all the fresh bread and cakes and left the stale ones. Otto sent the boy back home and went to sleep.

When Otto was awake—he usually managed to sit down behind the counter and look over the road into Tall Boy's shop until noon—he read newspapers from China which he got from friends in Port of Spain. He visited Tall Boy occasionally or Tall Boy came over to ask how business was going.

Tall Boy's desire was to acquire Otto's parlour, lock, stock, and barrel, at as low a price as possible. When he suggested that Otto wasn't doing well and should try his luck in the city, the sleepy-eyed, baby-faced Chinaman shook his head. He knew he would have to clear out, but it was not good business to agree with the suggestion. Tall Boy did not persist. He only kept an eye on Otto, and one morning he observed that business was slacking off too much, that perhaps he had better not invest in the parlour after all. Otto took alarm, and, seeing this, Tall Boy drove a hard bargain, saying that most of the goods in the shop were spoiled and old, and that he did not like the idea of losing money, he had many children to bring up. In the end Otto quit the district and bought a share in a Chinese restaurant in the city.

Tall Boy lost no time in taking down the sign over the entrance and putting up a new one proclaiming that the parlour was now his. He wrote on the wall with a piece of chalk: NO IDLARS ALLOWED. He stepped back, looked at his handiwork, and shook his head. He rubbed out the writing and wrote: IDLARS KEEP OUT.

He was busy to keep sales moving in both places. If he saw anyone going into the parlour he shouted, "Ah coming now!" and, calling out to Mary to attend in the shop, he ran across the road. This could not go on for any length of time. He was planning to move over all his stock and have the bar, shop, and parlour in one, as Otto's place was much bigger. But he decided for the time being that Mary and whichever of the children managed to stay away from school should remain in the parlour.

Tall Boy made fun with all the girls and young women in the village, even when Mary was present. She never paid attention to him laughing and leaning over the counter to touch their bodies. He told them, smiling, that he was going to sleep with them that night, and they said, "But this Tall Boy too fresh, *oui!* Yuh too fast wid yuhself!" When Mary was in the parlour he held their hands or commented on their figures, and in the bar he said to the men, "That is ah good one to sleep wid!" and the men laughed because they knew he was harmless. If the girls got angry he asked them if they couldn't take a joke. "Dou-dou, yuh know is only joke Ah making. Come, wat it is yuh want, butter? No butter dis week. No saltfish either."

The scales in the shop served a variety of purposes. Besides weighing the goods he sold, it also balanced fish, chickens, vegetables, and babies. Newly borns were taken to the shop to be weighed. With much ceremony Tall Boy would spread a clean sheet of paper and slip the pound along the notches. "Dat is ah good weight," he would admit, "but even Pewee weighed more wen he was born!" When fish or chicken venders passed and the villagers bought, they never trusted the weight until it was confirmed on Tall Boy's scales.

One morning there was great excitement in Barataria. Tall Boy got up and discovered that the shop had been broken into and a quantity of goods stolen. He spread the alarm, and two policemen came on bicycles from San Juan and took down a lot of notes in their books. Afterwards they went in the bar and had a drink. The whole neighbourhood sympathized with Tall Boy. Business continued as usual, but everyone had suggestions to offer; thieves had been prowling around in the nights lately, but Tall Boy was such a good man, he had done nobody wrong, it was a shame. In the evening he became reconciled, his mind warm with the concern of his neighbours, but with Mary it was a different thing. She wanted to know what the police were going to do about it, and how long it would take to bring the thieves to justice. She said they had better get a carpenter to reinforce all the doors in the parlour, so when they moved over no one would be tempted to break in. This Tall Boy did, supervising the work himself. One of the neighbours suggested that he get two big dogs, and as soon as he could he went to San Juan and procured two ferocious-looking animals from a hunter who assured him they would make good watchdogs.

The police never caught the thief or thieves, and after a few days the incident was forgotten and Tall Boy was ready to move over. Aware of the housing shortage, he planned to divide the shop into rooms and let them out. All the villagers wanted to move in, so he became choosy, looking around for a decent middle-class family. When one came he changed his mind and said he wanted only a couple, no children, and six months' rent in advance, to put in good flooring and paint the rooms. Two businessmen from San Juan offered to buy the premises, but Tall Boy was too smart to allow competition in the area if he could help it.

It was Joe Martin who got a tenant for him. Joe said it was a friend who was catching hell with some neighbours in Laventille, and who was willing to throw in a little reward together with the six months' rent. Tall Boy agreed, and Joe got the money for him. Once the money was in his hands Tall Boy didn't really care who came to live in the shop.

In order not to lose any business he decided to move over during a week-end. From the Saturday night he began taking over things himself, bit by bit, and all the children helped, and a few neighbours. Next morning a truck arrived, and the bulk of his stock was transported. The driver just backed the truck across the road up to the parlour and said it was the shortest trip he had ever taken. Tall Boy cut down this expense by offering the driver and loaders a drink. They drank a bottle and went away with another and three dollars for the job, which was a good deal.

Once settled in his new quarters, Tall Boy reckoned his assets and liabilities and, checking on those who owed him, announced that too many people were reducing the amounts they paid. He sat up one night and put the account book in order. He gathered all the slips of paper and sat down at the counter. He ticked here and there and grumbled now and again at an account long overdue. Joe Martin owed him twenty dollars for rum alone. Tiger hadn't paid last week—and yes, his wife had taken six pounds of flour that morning and he had forgotten to mark it. "Mary," he called, "anybody take anyting and yuh forget to mark it?" Mary came and together they went over the accounts.

Tall Boy was satisfied with his profits. He could send more money home to China. Mary wanted a new dress, but she had got one just six months ago, that could wait. He looked down at the khaki pants he wore. It had given him a year's constant service, with two others. Tall Boy was no miser, but he believed in cutting down expenses to a minimum. For one thing, he didn't need any clothes right now. He had had a suit cut on the latest American lines by a popular tailor in Port of Spain, which he sometimes wore on a Sunday when friends visited them, but apart from another tweed suit (it was regrettable that he had to travel once a week on business) that was all he felt need for. Khaki pants and white merino, just as most of the shopkeepers in the island wore, were enough for him. The clothes could wait. The children . . . he didn't have immediate plans for the future; the main thing was to have money for them when they grew up to open their own business . . . they could wait. But he had to pay the carpenter, and flour and rice were running low. And Mary was going to have another baby soon. He had heard how Rita delivered Urmilla's baby, though she was no midwife—perhaps she would help them when Mary's time came. It was worth a try, anyway; he would speak to Joe when next he came into the bar about the money he owed, and perhaps they could make a deal. And about the money Tiger owed, he would threaten not to pay for the milk if Tiger did not put something against the account. Fifty dollars' worth of goods went in the robbery. There was no way of getting it back: he would have to count it as a loss. It was a good thing he kept his money locked up in the house.

He switched off the lights after making sure that all the doors were properly bolted.

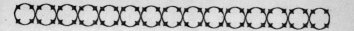

CHAPTER FIVE

Though the tentacles of war reached into the country districts as in the shortage of foodstuffs and the putting up of bases here and there, village folk plodded on in life and didn't worry about how the war was going. A man named Soylo who lived in the Northern Range, up on the Aripo hills in the central part of the island, didn't know there was a war on until a day in August 1942. And when he heard he shrugged his shoulders and said, "O-ho! Dat is why we seeing so much trouble to get saltfish in de shop now!" But when he heard about submarines and bombs he got nervous and wanted to know if the Germans were coming to bomb Trinidad. Soylo used to grow vegetables and load his donkey and walk over the hills to sell in the villages in the valley. He was so scared about the war talk that he left the village and went right back into the hills. And every time he heard the sound of an airplane he ran into the bush to hide. One day he saw an airplane towing a target. He didn't know what it was; he was so frightened he went into his hut and barricaded the door and didn't come out for the whole day, just kept his hands over his ears, waiting for the bombs to fall. People in Port of Spain might worry when a tanker carrying precious oil from the refineries in Point-à-Pierre was torpedoed just off the coast, but what did it matter to the villagers as long as nothing happened to the land, and crops came and cattle thrived on the green grass, and their bellies were filled? News that the enemy had retreated was treated in the same manner as news of an adverse advance.

The war was so distant from them they could even joke about it in Tall Boy's shop. "But yuh ain't get saltfish yet? Is wat happen? Dey bomb de ship dat was bringing it from England?" And when there was no saltfish, didn't they have tomatoes and beans and cabbages growing out of the rich earth? Even in peace they hadn't bothered much about the outside world; there were some old Indians in Barataria who had never been to the city, just four miles away.

Tiger knew something big was happening, men were killing each other for something. He used to wonder if he were out there in the bigness if he'd grow wise, if he'd learn more about life. Sometimes, in the morning when he got up early and dew was still heavy on the grass, he used to watch at what he could see of the world—the sky, light blue with promise of a sunlit day, the low hills that break away from the Northern Range and run hunchbacked for some miles, and the trees on the hills, dark green before the sun rose and made them lighter. With all this—with the mango tree in his yard, the flowers Urmilla had planted, the land he could see around, and gardens, he felt a certain satisfaction, as if he were living in accordance with the way things should live. These sensations happened too when he was working in the fields. Sometimes the sun burned into him so he raised his back and tried to look at it, knowing there was power and bigness there.

He used to spend hours in the shop, listening to opinion from the few who showed passing interest in how the battle waged. He usually kept silent and listened. He soon realized that with their tongues loosened over a bottle of rum they just talked and argued to pass time away, and he would learn nothing.

Among those who argued was an old Indian called Sookdeo.
Sookdeo lived on rum and memories. He was a little man, so
dark that his grey beard and straggly hair seemed growing out
of his face. His legs were bowed, varicose veins ran crazily on
them. His hands were cracked and gnarled with labour—his
whole body gave that impression, as if he had done too much
work in his childhood, before his bones had a chance to shapen
themselves. His cheeks were sunken and tough, his eyes small
and red and piercing. Sookdeo still had two teeth in his mouth
with which he could rip the skin off a piece of sugar cane with
ease; with them and his hardened gums he could eat anything.
If he laughed, and he often did, the teeth were like brown ugly
stubs set in chocolate blancmange. He had come from India to
work as an indentured labourer on the white man's plantations.
He liked to talk about how it was with him, about the old days.
How he had worked himself to the bone. How he used to
seduce girls in the canefields. How he had lived in San Juan
when the land was planted with cane, and not as it was today,
with houses and streets. He remembered when the whole of
Barataria was cultivating cane, spreading down to the swamp.
And if he got encouragement in the form of a drink, he would
go on to relate how he had married and fathered two girls.
That was when he took to rum, because after that his wife
could bear no more children, and he had wanted a boy child.

Sookdeo lived in a broken-down hut which he was always
promising Rookmin, his wife, to repair. But he was never sober
enough to do it. Every day, every night, it was the same question he asked in the hut—when was Dolly and Seta going to get
married and relieve him of the responsibility of having to feed
them?

And why yuh don't go and make ah match, den? Rookmin
wanted to know. Why yuh don't go San Juan or Tacarigua and
get two man for dem?

Eventually it was Rookmin who fixed up a marriage for Seta. It was a scrappy sort of affair, because they were too poor to have any ceremony. All Sookdeo did was to get some red clay and stamp hand-prints all over the walls of the hut, and put up a long bamboo with a red flag in the yard. Then he filled a basket with tomatoes from his garden and sold them and bought a bottle of rum. He was drunk for three days, celebrating the wedding in his own way. When he came to his senses Seta was gone.

"Is only you dere now, Dolly," he said to his daughter, "but you stay dis side little wile, you does cookam good, make good roti. Stay little longer wid *bap*, and help yuh *mai*."

Every day, but especially on Saturdays and Sunday mornings, all the farmers in and around Barataria brought their produce on the roadside to sell. The market was a strip of asphalt about one hundred yards long, leading from the Eastern Main Road into the village. Here Joseph, the butcher, a red-faced half-Spaniard, sold meat at black-market prices. Most of the rich people in Port of Spain came on Sunday mornings to buy from Joseph, because by prearrangement he kept the choice cuts for them, and they paid whatever he asked. What remained he sold to the villagers. His stall was always crowded with customers demanding their half-pounds and one pounds; Joseph used to make the half-pounds wait until last. It was a clamour and a pushing, and no one dared to ask the price, they just thrust money in his hands and took what change they got and considered themselves lucky. "But Mr. Joseph! So long Ah here waiting for dis half-pound beef, and yuh serving dem people before me!" "Mr. Joseph, please tanks for ah half-pound?" And Joseph would pause and calmly sharpen his knife, working his elbows and looking at the customers with a glassy stare. Sometimes when the noise was too much he leaned on the back of the stall and folded his arms, refusing to serve until some order was restored.

Fisherwomen occupied the left side of the road near the concrete culvert. They sold only to customers they knew, because once one of them—Matilda—had kicked up a big noise when a man didn't want to pay what she asked, and it had led to trouble: the magistrate in Port of Spain fined her two hundred dollars. While Joseph charged black-market prices quite openly—he was friendly with the police, and it was rumoured that he occasionally bribed them—the fisherwomen whispered in the ears of customers that things were bad with them, they had to pay high prices for the fish in the city, and transport it to the village, and not to let anyone see them passing the money.

The vegetable vendors spread old bags on the right side of the road and laid out their cassava and dasheen and peas. Sookdeo had a special spot at the head of the road where he did his selling. Somehow his crops were always plentiful, though he hardly did any work in his garden. While the others rose early and worked until the sun went down, Sookdeo would be straying about the village, trying to get a drink of rum. While they planted by the seasons and were anxious when the rains did not come, he just pushed seeds in the soil. It seemed the earth returned his careless love for it and sent his plants up into the sunlight while others were employing manure and chemicals for their seeds to sprout.

Sookdeo was not a good vendor. He teased the people who came to buy and ogled at the women and girls. After an hour or so, when perhaps he had sold a shilling's worth, he would go out on the main road for a drink. If he met company he would forget all about selling.

Sookdeo never remained in one spot. He moved around

from vendor to vendor, mocking the size of their vegetables, playfully cursing some of them. He had a sense of humour which enabled him to be always laughing at people, as if life was a huge joke, not to be treated seriously, the best way out was to be drunk as often and as long as possible. If sales were dull he lowered his prices despite the protests from all sides. He would walk bow-legged up and down the street with a few bunches of lettuce, bawling out, "Takeam watever you giveam for it!" Sometimes he got so drunk on the money he made that he rolled in the street, laughing and kicking his legs in the air. Or he rolled in the gutter and lay still, all gone. Then someone would tell Rookmin, and she would send Dolly to drag him home.

The whole of Barataria knew Sookdeo and humoured him on in life, knowing it was not going to be long before he died from rum—or lack of it. He swaggered in the knowledge that he was popular, and when he was really broke didn't think anything of begging, screwing up his face in a woebegone expression. "Is only to buy rum yuh want money, Sookdeo," they told him. And he wouldn't deny it.

In the rainy season, when bushes and grass grew high in yards, he offered to hoe and cutlass. He would ask for part payment before he started and go off and get drunk and not return for days. "Aaye, you Sookdeo! Don't play yuh don't know me! Don't bend down yuh head, Ah see is you already! Yuh take me money, and up to now yuh ain't come to weed de yard! Ah bet yuh Ah call ah policeman for yuh!" And Sookdeo would clutch his back as if in great pain and say, "Too much sick dis side, pain all over body. But me come tomorrow please God."

He was the butt of the children. They were afraid of him and teased from a distance. "Sookdeo! Yuh old drunkard!" They ran when he waved his cutlass or hoe threateningly.

When the children misbehaved at home their parents threatened to give them to Sookdeo, and that made them quiet.

Sookdeo could read. He always read the *Trinidad Guardian* for Tall Boy, who wanted to find out what was happening in China. Customers were always talking about the acute water shortage in Laventille, or how the government was tightening up restrictions on the waterfront, or something which did not interest him greatly. With all that he felt he did not properly belong; it was only when Sookdeo read the news about China that he sat down and leaned over the counter.

"Plenty trouble in China now, Sookdeo?"

The old Indian would grunt and peer at the front page. He would have liked to read the news himself and then tell Tall Boy in his own words, but the Chinaman didn't trust him. He felt Sookdeo's interpretation would be wrong, he wanted the printed words read out aloud, one by one. And this also gave him the satisfaction that Sookdeo worked for the drink with which he had to be supplied to clear his throat. Sookdeo would put his forefinger under each word and call it out, and Tall Boy would say yes, yes, and nod his head. Sometimes there was local news about certain commodities being short, or prices had gone up. After Sookdeo read these Tall Boy would clip the news and paste it on a piece of cardboard and hang it where all the customers could see. Often, when Tall Boy wasn't looking, Sookdeo would skip a line or a paragraph and chuckle to himself. It became a habit that every morning on his way to the fields he would stop to read the papers and have his first drink—an "eye-opener," he called it. After a time he reflected newspaper opinion and would put an end to arguments by saying he had read it in the *Guardian*.

Besides his gardening, Sookdeo made money by doing odd jobs with his donkey cart. There was no job of transportation which he did not offer to do. If someone was moving a short distance from one house to another, Sookdeo brought the cart and offered to move the furniture. If anyone was ill and wanted to go to San Juan to see a doctor, he rigged up a covering with old rice bags to keep off the glare of the sun and offered the services of his cart. But he never ventured into Port of Spain. He said the traffic was too heavy, that he might get in an accident. But the truth was that he had never been to the capital and was afraid; it would be like going into a strange new land. San Juan was all right, he could get drunk there and people he knew would see that he got home.

When the donkey wasn't working he turned it loose in the savannah opposite the government school. Children playing there used to stone it until Sookdeo ran down a boy with his cutlass. Dolly took a bucket of water for it at midday and went back in the evening to bring it home. Sookdeo's only interest in the animal was in the work it could do. He used to call it "Donkey." In the morning he said, "Donkey, get up," and in the evening, "Donkey, lay down." Donkey was a faithful beast. He had brought his master home safely after many a drunken spree in the rumshop, and once, coming in one of the back streets from San Juan, Sookdeo had fallen off and he had stood by him for three hours until somebody passed and put Sookdeo back on the cart.

But one rainy night Donkey fell ill. Sookdeo had gone into a rumshop and left the animal out in the rain for hours.

The next morning, when Sookdeo said, "Donkey, get up," Donkey refused to budge. It was the first time such a thing happened. "But a-a, me tellam you get up nar, Donkey!" But the animal just looked at Sookdeo with watery eyes.

"Dolly! eh gul, is wat you doam Donkey, he don't get up?"

The girl came running out of the hut. "*Bap*, Ah tink Donkey sick."

Rookmin followed her. "Yuh don't take care of Donkey, is how yuh expect him to be well all de time?"

From that day Donkey wouldn't work any more. He just shuffled about the yard, munching hibiscus leaves which Dolly cut from fences in the streets, and Sookdeo thought that the animal had gone blind.

A few days later Sookdeo decided to sell Donkey. Ramdhin, a young Indian, wanted a donkey cart to sell coconuts in Port of Spain. Sookdeo brought him home to see Donkey.

"Him fat, him doam plenty work and eatam little, but him don't 'look' well," Sookdeo said.

Ramdhin looked at Donkey. "Yuh cud see ribs, man, de donkey look half-dead. Is how much yuh tink Ah going to give yuh for him?"

Sookdeo shrugged. "Well, is true dat he old, but him cud still do plenty hard work. Is only dat him don't 'look' well."

"How yuh mean him don't look well?"

"Well, look dat side for yuhself, nar. Him don't 'look' well."

"He look plenty sick, if dat is wat yuh mean. I go give yuh fifty dollar."

"Boy, talkam nonsense! Donkey cud tote plenty coconut. Him don't get tired quick, is only dat him don't 'look' well. Giveam sixty dollar, nar?"

"For dat half-dead donkey? Man, look, is fifty dollar or nutting."

Visions of inexhaustible supplies of rum floated in Sookdeo's mind. He might even be able to pay off Tall Boy some money and give Rookmin five dollars for herself and Dolly.

"All right, giveam fifty dollar," he agreed. And as Ramdhin was leading Donkey away he called out, "Remember me tellam him don't 'look' well, but him work hard!"

He had hardly entered the hut before Rookmin asked him how much money he had got for Donkey.

Sookdeo thought swiftly and fumbled in his pocket and brought out two ten-dollar bills. "Only twenty dollar him give, him say Donkey look half-dead."

Rookmin snatched a bill from his fingers before he could move. "Well dis one is mine," she said triumphantly; "at least Tall Boy go get some money. We must be owe him plenty."

Sookdeo made a great show of protest and made as if he were going to pull at Rookmin, but she pushed the bill down in her bosom and then dared him to try and get it, and Dolly begged them not to fight.

The next morning just as he got his cutlass and hoe and was setting off for the fields Ramdhin came up.

Ramdhin was enraged, and for a minute he cursed Sookdeo steadily in Hindi. Then he broke out in broken English.

"But look here, Sookdeo, wat yuh mean by selling me ah half-blind donkey?"

Sookdeo feigned astonishment. "But me tellam him fat, him work hard, but him don't 'look' well."

Ramdhin choked. "But yuh is ah damn fool! Yuh can't even explain yuhself! Why yuh didn't tell me de donkey blind?"

"But me tellam! Me say him fat, but him don't 'look' well. Yuh don't understand when me talkam good English give yuh?"

"Look, Ah can't work de donkey if he half-blind," Ramdhin said. "Yuh go have to give me back me money."

"Talkam mad! Me have nutting more to do wid yuh, business finish, me sellam you one donkey dis side, you buy."

"Yuh is ah damn tief!"

It wasn't very long before the story ran the length and breadth of the village. Sookdeo himself began the spreading, having rested his tools in a corner of the shop and called for a bottle of rum.

As he proffered a five-dollar bill the Chinaman gasped. "Where yuh get dat money, Sookdeo?"

And Sookdeo told the story, between drinks, and those in the shop heard it and it was a big joke, they forgot all about reading the newspapers.

It was almost midday when the bottle of rum was finished. Sookdeo had told Tall Boy not to worry, that Rookmin would pay off some money on what they owed, and Tall Boy suggested that he save the money he had. "Put some money in de bank, man," he said.

"Wat bank? Best bank in de world is dis side," and Sookdeo patted his pocket.

"But yuh sure to drink out all dat money. Let me keep it for you, and wen yuh want Ah will give yuh," Tall Boy urged, for he didn't like the idea of Sookdeo drinking it all away and owing him all over again.

But Sookdeo was thinking about what Tall Boy said. He had never had so much money at one time in his life. He kept his hand in his pocket and played with the bills, feeling like he supposed a man with a lot of money would feel. But Tall Boy was right. When Rookmin paid him he could always trust a bottle now and then. But what should he do with the money? He couldn't keep it on him all the time; by now Rookmin must have found out how much he really got for Donkey and was only waiting a chance to rifle his pockets. His eyes roamed the shop as he thought, and alighted on a shelf with tins.

Suddenly he knew what he was going to do. He asked Tall Boy for an empty Ovaltine tin.

"Wat yuh want to do wid it?"

"Nothing, man. Neighbour ask me bringam dry ochro seed for she to plant, so me go puttam in de tin."

When Sookdeo left the shop he was walking as if he had not had a touch of rum for the morning. In his garden he looked

around to see if anybody was near. His plot of land adjoined
Tiger's; he could see the young man, his back was bent, he was
planting. Sookdeo crouched and a clump of black sagebush
hid him from view. He sat down on the ground, between two
banks of tomatoes, and took the money from his pocket. Sunlight struck the paper and the bills glared. Sookdeo had never
read what was written on a bill. But now he spread them out
on the ground, rubbing out the creases, and reading slowly
what the Treasury people write on bills.

When they were all smooth he folded them small and put
them in the Ovaltine tin. Where should he bury it? In one of
the beds? No, Rookmin and Dolly sometimes came in the garden and in weeding might uncover it. The spot must be one
on which no work would ever be done. He looked at a long
mango tree which grew right on the border of his plot. Still
bending low, he went to it and selected a spot between two
roots. He dug deep with the cutlass, until perspiration bathed
his body. Still he dug, looking around anxiously every now
and then to make sure no one was watching. Then he put in
the tin and covered it with a dry piece of wood. He filled the
hole, taking a risk of being seen by standing to stamp the earth
firmly in. He shovelled dry leaves with his foot and scattered
them over the spot. Then he swung his cutlass carelessly at
the mango tree and made a deep gash in the trunk to mark
the spot, and sap ran out.

Two days later the sap turned into a brown, gluey substance,
with a blob where it stopped running down the trunk.

Tiger had often seen Sookdeo sitting on a bag of rice, reading the papers in the shop, his eyes squinted as if he were looking at the sun. And though they exchanged words, he was too
shy to strengthen the acquaintanceship. He was always promising himself to ask Sookdeo questions, because he could read

and he would know so many things—about the war, about other lands and how people lived. Perhaps Sookdeo might even teach him to read, and then he could borrow books and magazines and his mind would become big as he read of the world and the seas.

One morning no customers were in the shop, and Tall Boy was opening a barrel of saltfish in the back. Only Sookdeo was there, digging between his toes with one hand and tracing words on the sheet of paper with the other. Tiger made up his mind. Two things would win the old man's favour—respect and rum. He got to the point right away.

"Mr. Sookdeo," he said, "all these things you does read about, you think you could tell me, how ships sinking, and why people fighting war, and all that sort of thing?"

It seemed as if Sookdeo didn't hear him at first. Then slowly the paper was lowered and the old Indian looked at Tiger. He burst into great cackling laughter. "Is wat you callam me, boy? *Mr.* Sookdeo?"

"Is nothing wrong in that," Tiger said uneasily.

Sookdeo got down from the rice bag and put his arms around Tiger. He could not remember the last time he had been treated with such respect. Even the children laughed at him. It was always "Aaye" or "baboo" or just plain "Sookdeo." The occasion was worthy of a drink. He called to Tall Boy.

Tiger didn't want to surprise his stomach with a drink so early in the morning, but he couldn't refuse Sookdeo. He paid for a nip, and after they drank Sookdeo asked him exactly what it was he wanted to find out.

But Tiger couldn't explain the way he felt about things. Even after Sookdeo read the latest news for him, it was as nothing. He heard, and imagined how it was in England and America. But he was conscious only of the great distance which separated him from all that was happening. Things always happened to other people, but nothing happened to him. Only big responsibility. He was disappointed. He had expected that as soon as Sookdeo explained things, the knowledge would put him right. But the more he listened—and Sookdeo flavoured the facts with his own opinion—the more perplexed he became.

Tiger decided to go to his garden, and Sookdeo took the rum and went with him, though he said it was a bad thing to drink rum in the hot sun, but he couldn't talk much unless his throat was wet.

Sookdeo sat down and watched Tiger plant tomato seeds. Once in his garden, Tiger became engrossed in cleaning his beds and forgot all about the conversation. For some weeks now he had been waging a losing battle with a persistent type of weed, which the gardeners called "Mary-shut-you-gate" because when the leaves were touched they folded in. He was tired weeding them out—they sprang up again every three or four days. What used to anger him a lot was when he looked over at Sookdeo's plot of land and saw his crops growing though weeds were thick on the ground, and Sookdeo was never doing any work, turning up the soil or cutlassing or anything, like now, sitting down there and drinking rum.

"But, Sookdeo, how it is you crops always coming good and you don't do work in the garden, man?"

"Is who tell yuh me nar doam work? Yuh tink things cud grow just so, unless you help dem?"

"But, man, I does be working hard here every day, and I does scarcely see you; it look as if the only time I see you is when you reaping crop, not planting them. And too besides, look at the state of you garden. Man, black sage and Mary-shut-you-gate growing all about, as if that is what you plant!"

Sookdeo tilted the bottle to his head and took a long drink; amber in the bottle reflected yellow in the sunlight. "Listen, boy, Ah cud see yuh still young. Yuh have plenty tings to learn. In de first place, yuh have to love de tings yuh plant."

"Is how you mean?"

"Ah can't explain. Is just dat yuh must love de tomatoes and lettuce and pigeon peas, and dey go grow if yuh love dem. And in de second place, yuh have to know which crop to plant, and wen."

Tiger dug deeply at a root. "Well, I does love the tings I plant," he said sullenly. "I does like to see them growing up, and when flowers come, and then I does take good care. Well, the crops and them does be good, but what I want to know is how you don't even do half of what I does do, and yet yours come good too? It have a agriculture man from the government does come round sometimes, and give we advice, because it have war, you know, and they say we must grow more food. You does do what he tell you to do? Is that why you crops always good?"

"Yuh mean dat fella who come dis side? He smart. He know what he talkam bout, he have plenty book knowledge. One time, yuh know, he come and ask me how Ah does plant, and why Ah don't take more care wid de garden. Dat time Ah was planting pigeon peas. He look at de young trees and he tell me dat unless Ah do wat he say, Ah wouldn't get enough peas to feed ah fowl. But yuh tink Ah worry wid him? Nar, man. Two, three month after he come back, and dis time so, pigeon peas laden on de trees, boy, until de branches touching de ground. He look and he say is ah good ting Ah do wat he say, and Ah keep quiet and say yes, but Ah didn't follow he advice at all, and yet Ah had peas like fire. Ah must be makeam bout twenty dollar dat season."

"Well, that is you, but I well follow the advice he give me, and my lettuce coming good."

"If yuh want, Ah teach yuh one, two ting."

"Like what so? You won't say you know more than government people!"

"Haveam some ting yuh learn only by experience."

A cart laden with manure, drawn by a sleepy-eyed ox, came slowly along the trail. The driver shouted, "Tiger! Yuh wife ask me to drop dis manure here for yuh!"

"Is you Boysie? Bring the cart up near, man, I want it just over here."

Boysie guided the heavy-footed ox skilfully between two beds of lettuce. He looked at Sookdeo and shook his head. "Yuh mustn't drink modder's milk in de hot sun, man," he said. But he got off the cart and had a drink himself.

Tiger hoed the cattle dung off the cart. "Leave some for me," Boysie said, "just little bit. Ah want to manure some ochro tree."

Boysie was a handsome Indian, strong and straight and popular with the girls. He had his own plot of land and worked hard. Nearly every night he was in Port of Spain having a good time, learning all the latest American songs, which he sang and whistled when at work. He had been in a city grocery for a number of years until one Christmas Eve when he tried to steal six bottles of wine. The boss said he wouldn't call the police but he had to leave the job. After that he couldn't get another job, so he turned to the land. But his mind was always in the city; he didn't like the slow Indian ways of life he saw around him in the village, and lately he had been thinking seriously of going away to America, or England, and turn over a new leaf. But Stella, the Negro girl friend he had in Port of Spain, told him to wait until the war was over. So he had begun to save his money.

Boysie was mixed up good and proper with the cosmopolitan atmosphere of the city and was at home with anybody. The few Indian friends he had were men; he didn't like Indian girls, he said they were too passive in their love-making, that the best woman he had ever had was a creole. For this reason he was not liked by the elderly Indians in the village, but Boysie didn't care. He used to say that all this business about colour and nationality was balls, that as long as a man was happy that was all that mattered. He got a delight out of seeing the stares of deep-rooted Indians when he walked around the Queen's Park Savannah with Stella holding on to his arm. "Look at dem," he used to say, "dey so stupid, is as if Ah committing ah crime. Girl, yuh happy?" and when Stella nodded—"Well, I happy too. Is why everybody can't live good together?" He walked in Park Street and Frederick Street, and whenever he saw a couple of different nationalities he used to hail out to them and tell Stella that that was the way to live, especially in Trinidad.

Tiger liked Boysie because of his freedom. Sometimes he talked of life in the city, and it was a new world to Tiger, who had never seen a trolley-bus or a tram, or the house the Governor lived in, or the Red House where the politicians held their meetings. Boysie had promised to take him to the city and show him the sights. As he hoed the manure into a compact heap so the sun wouldn't dry it quickly, he reminded Boysie of this.

"When you going to town again, Boysie?"

"Eh-eh, yuh foot getting hot since Ah tell yuh bout dat, eh! Wat about Saturday? We cud spend de whole day—if yuh have money."

"I want to go by the sea and see the ships."

Sookdeo made a disgusted sound with his teeth and tongue. "Wat yuh goam town to see? Yuh cud get plenty rum dis side, right by Tall Boy.'

"Don't mind he, Tiger," Boysie said, "as long as he cud get

ah bottļe ah rum, dat is all he want. He don't know dey have oder tings in de world."

Sookdeo stuck the empty bottle on a limb of bamboo. "All right, allyuh is young, but I gettam old already," and he went away to another part of the fields to find more agreeable company.

"Tell me about the time when the Governor did come, Boysie."

"Ah tell yuh bout dat already, man. It was ah big ting. People like fire, lining de road to see him, and de police band playing, and guards and soldiers. He went to de Red House and make ah speech. Dey had all dem big shots dere. Opposite in Woodford Square it had ah loudspeaker running from de Red House, and we cud hear everyting de new Governor saying, bout wat he going to do to make Trinidad ah better place."

"What about the house he live in? Is a big house?"

"Dat is house fadder, boy! Is de biggest house in Trinidad. It have policemen guarding it. It have ah hundred window! One time ah rich man in San Fernando did build ah house wid one hundred window, and dey make him take out one, because dey say is only de Governor house must have ah hundred window in it. So yuh can imagine."

Tiger imagined. What he didn't know hurt him more than what he knew.

Boysie said, "Ah going to manure de ochro tree, man. Ah will see yuh on Saturday, den. Pass to meet yuh?"

"Yes, man. I will wait home for you. You know the place?"

"But how? Ain't is next to Joe? About nine o'clock. We must go early as stores closing half-day."

A cloud shaped like a magnified amoeba passed under the sun, and Tiger watched its shadow on the ground coming towards him. He sat down to rest but the shade only lasted a minute and the cloud moved on. He was wet with perspiration;

he was not in the habit of drinking rum in the forenoon, and the added heat had him uncomfortable. He unbuttoned his torn shirt and turned his bare chest to a passing breeze.

Life was beginning to get complicated, now that he was beginning to learn things. Sookdeo had promised to teach him to read. Boysie was going to show him many things in Port of Spain. Where was his life going to fit in? Perhaps, if he liked the city, he could get a job there, and give up the garden. Or Urmilla could keep it while he was at work. Anyway, he wasn't sure. He wasn't sure about anything. He would just have to wait until the time came. Maybe he'd see some sign, or have a dream telling him exactly what to do. One night he had dreamed that Mary-shut-you-gate had grown all over his beds and stifled the young trees. Next morning the baby was ill, gasping as if she couldn't breathe. The dream was right, only it had happened to his child and not his garden. When he was out in the open many thoughts came to him. He tried always to follow the sequence of circumstances which had befallen him since he left Chaguanas; it seemed years ago. Sometimes a heart-slowing homesickness overcame him, and he wanted to run back into his life as a boy in the canefields, with no thoughts to worry him, with parents to give him food and occasionally short khaki pants to wear. How easy it had been to get up and milk the cows or fix the harness on the mules, and go to work with the others, talking about games and who had the most marbles. He remembered once, playing a game of "hoop," he had got lost in the cane. Right in the middle of the field he went to hide, and when he wanted to come out he didn't know in which direction to turn. The way he felt then, it was the same when he cowered under the shadow of life now. When Urmilla and the baby were asleep he looked up at the roof and felt revulsion for his wife and child. They were to blame for all his worry. If he were alone he could be like Boysie, not caring a damn. He would go to the city and get a job—not just an ordinary job, like how Boysie used to work in a grocery, but something bigger. He would even go to school in the night and learn to read and write. Right here in Barataria he could have gone to school, but everybody would laugh at a big married man like him going to class with a slate and pencil. Even little Henry could read and write a little. Every time he thought of that Tiger winced as if he had been slapped in the face. True, Joe himself couldn't write, and he had said he could live without it. But he was no old man, to resign himself to a poor life, killing out his body in the fields, spending so much money to buy some kind of special food Rita had told Urmilla was good for the baby. Look at Sookdeo, he argued, you think I want to be like he when I get old? Is only old age that I respect in him. All he could do is read and drink rum. When I learn to read, you think is only *Guardian* I going to read? I going to read plenty books, about America and England, and all them places. Man, I will go and live in Port of Spain; this village too small, you can't learn anything except how to plant crop.

So the tune went on in his brain. Out in the open there was plenty space and trees, and when he raised his head he could see the hills of the Northern Range and feel himself a part of it all. And he found satisfaction in the growth of the seeds he planted. From the time he put them in the black earth, adding a little manure, he kept close vigil for the first signs. And when the seeds burst and the shoots peeped at the sun, he felt that at least he could make things grow, if even he didn't have any knowledge. As the tomato trees grew he put brambles and small branches to support them, and watched the flowers, tiny and yellow; and then the fruit, in the beginning pale and at times shrunken, but swelling out and attaining a healthy green, to ripen red and rosy under the sun, and sell for a shilling a pound in the market or at a cut rate if he sold wholesale to a vender. Urmilla liked to be with him when the trees were bearing. She was of little help but her company was welcome; he felt good showing her what he had done. They had always thought the fruit came out of the earth in the night to grow on the branches, until the day the man from the agricultural department explained about pollination. Neither of them understood properly, but Tiger saw the wonder of it and grew to love the land more.

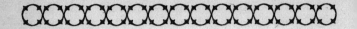

CHAPTER SIX

When Tiger told Urmilla he was going to Port of Spain she begged to be taken along. But he said just he and Boysie were going, and she would be a hindrance to their activities. But he promised to buy a bonnet for the baby.

"Go in one of the big store, Tiger, and get a good one. Rita say that it have a store by the corner of Queen and Frederick Street which part you could get plenty things to buy," Urmilla told him. And when Boysie passed to meet him and they were about to leave, "Mind you don't get knock down with car, you know how traffic busy in town!"

Boysie laughed. "Yuh won't say he is a small boy and can't take care of himself!"

They walked out to the Eastern Main Road. Tiger had put on a clean white shirt. Boysie had on a jitterbug shirt with palms and birds.

"Is how we going, by bus?"

"Man, taxi is only six cents more. We will reach town in two-twos, dem old bus too slow."

Transportation between the city and most districts on the main road was not difficult. A private company ran a regular though dilapidated bus service, which was competed against by hundreds of flashy American cars. Once an Indian bought

84

an old English make, which looked like a tortoise among the other cars in the car-stand in George Street. The other drivers gave him a lot of jokes, asking him why he didn't take "dat ol' dus'bin" off the road. But while they were charging double the bus fare, the Indian used to get more passengers by offering to take them for a penny less. This made him very unpopular with the other taximen and eventually led to a fight. It started when a Negro driver, trying to manoeuvre his taxi near to the corner of Queen and George Streets, a strategic spot to "block" passengers, scraped the fender of the English car.

"Is why yuh don't get dat damn ol' tin pan from de road, Persuad? Yuh don't see yuh blocking de way?"

"But look at dis man, nar! Look at trouble here today! Yuh best hads make up yuh mind yuh have to buy ah new fender for me."

One word led to another, and Persuad came out of his car and cursed the Negro's ancestors, and the Negro hauled a jack from under his front seat. They caused considerable interest to vendors and passers-by, who joined in the cries of "Beat 'im! Beat 'im up!" meaning any one of the two. They were brought to court and deemed rogues and vagabonds and fined one hundred dollars each. As Persuad couldn't bear the shame of going to jail he had to sell his car to pay the fine. He got two hundred dollars for it, which was more than he had expected, and after paying the fine went to drive a big Mack truck for the Americans down at one of the bases.

The taxi Tiger and Boysie were in stopped twice to pick up passengers. The driver asked Boysie where he was getting off, and when he said by the railway station, the driver decided he could risk overloading with two more, and an old Negro woman with a basket of fish came in and sat between Tiger and Boysie.

"Listen, man," Boysie told the driver, "wat slackness is dis?

Ah bet yuh we get out and take anoder taxi! Dis old woman come to smell me up wid fish!"

"Is why yuh making so much fuss for, pardner? Ah only trying to make a little extra money. Yuh see how it is we people can't get on! Man, yuh is ah Indian like myself!"

"Ah ain't have nutting to do wid dat, nar. Is eider dis woman come out de car, or me and my pardner take anoder car."

"Look, Ah tell yuh wat. I go put de fish in de trunk behind," and the driver took the basket from the woman, who was glaring at Boysie. He started off again quickly before Boysie could say anything.

"Ah wish ah policeman cud hold yuh up for overloading," Boysie grumbled as they got under way. He turned to the woman. "And is why yuh looking at me so, *macoumere?* Yuh don't like me face?"

She looked out the window and didn't say a word.

Boysie turned to Tiger. "Boy, dese taximen does have tings their own way too much. Some of dem does tell yuh dey leaving right away, and wen yuh get in de car, is because dey making rounds all Charlotte Street for more passengers, and wat yuh cud do? Nothing, because yuh in de car already. As for wen dey going down south! Boy, dat is trouble self. All dem touts by de railway station, from de time dey see yuh wid ah grip in yuh hand, dey start hustling. 'South, mister? Yuh going south? Look ah nice car here—it have radio. Leaving right away. South direct.' And dis time de smart driver have bout three tout sitting down quiet as if dey is passengers. Is only wen yuh get in, and he lock up yuh grip in de trunk, and begin to make rounds—all down Park Street, all round by Piccadilly and Green Corner—dat yuh realize yuh get stick, and yuh wouldn't be leaving for south until he get four more passenger."

The taxi halted by the railway station, and Boysie and Tiger got out. "Pay de man, is only ah shilling," he told Tiger.

Tiger said, "Man, I haven't any change. A five dollar is the smallest change I have."

"A-a, but yuh holding big! Well, see if de driver have change."

But the driver hadn't, and they had to get in and go to Marine Square, where Tiger went into a restaurant and asked for change, but the attendant refused unless he bought something, so Boysie said to take a packet of cigarettes.

When they paid the driver he said to Boysie, "Boy, dat is two good drive yuh had in my taxi. De first and de last. Never me and yuh again!"

And as the car drove off the old woman poked her head out of the window and shouted, "Yuh nasty coolie! I smelling of fish, but wat you smelling of?" The rest of her words was inaudible as the car swung into George Street.

Boysie only laughed and told Tiger the best way to start the day was to have a drink. They had a nip in Columbus Bar, and Tiger felt much better.

As they were near the waterfront Boysie suggested that they take a walk along the wharf. Above the roofs of the storage sheds they could see the masts of ocean-going steamers. "Some of dem is passenger boat, but a lot is tankers come for oil to carry to England. And oders come for sugar. Dey have plenty ships here because from all down by South America dey come here and meet, and den all of dem go over de sea together, in a ting dey call convoy. Dat way, it harder for submarine to attack dem."

"Why it harder?"

"Well, yuh damn fool, ain't it easier to beat one man dan to beat two?"

"How long it does take to reach England?"

"Ah don't know, man, bout two or three week. But one day"
—and Boysie's voice fell, as if he were speaking to himself—
"wen de war over, Ah going America. On one of dem ship
self. Yuh can't imagine how life different dere, boy."

"But how you know?"

"Man, yuh forget, Ah born in de city here. We don't grow
up chu-chut and foolish like allyuh in de country. We could
see plenty pictures in de theatres, and read books from de
library, and talk to people who went dere already."

"So tell me something, Boysie, when I used to work in the
canefield, and help make sugar, it went to England too?"

"Yes, man."

"You think the people who eating sugar over there does
think about we who making it here?"

"You does tink bout who make de shoes yuh wearing?"

"Yes, I does wonder about which part it come from, and
how the cow was in the field grazing, and then they kill it, and
put the skin to dry, and then how people in the factories make
shoes."

"Well, everybody ain't have time like you to bodder wid
dem tings, yuh see. I for one don't want to know which part
it come from, as long as Ah cud get it."

"But man, Boysie, you must be interested in things."

Boysie looked at Tiger as if he were seeing him for the first
time. "Yuh shoudda been ah scholar instead of planting
tomatoes!"

"Boy, one day I going to get education and come a big man
in this country, boy. I going to be like big shot people in the
Red House—is which part the Red House is?"

"Let we go up de road, Ah go show yuh."

They crossed Marine Square and entered St. Vincent Street.
A tram-car went by, but Tiger felt it would be ridiculous to

ask Boysie about it. But he looked at it until it went up the street out of sight, clanging on the rails.

"Dat is de post office"—Boysie indicated a large building on his left, and a little higher up—"that is de *Guardian* office, and opposite is de *Gazette*. And just by de corner have ah rumshop. My throat dry answering all dese questions."

"But I never know they had *Gazette* papers."

"Well, yuh know now."

"So how they does get all the news and thing?"

"Man, yuh asking some funny questions, *oui*. Dey have reporters who does go out and collect news. Ah had ah good friend working at de *Guardian*, Ah wonder if he dere now. Ah sure he would come and chop one wid we."

They stood up on the pavement and looked up at the *Guardian* building and Boysie whistled long and loud. But after a minute he shrugged and told Tiger that his friend must have gone out to cover a story. "He is ah smart fellar, he have plenty education, he coudda tell yuh a lot of tings," he said.

They drank a nip in Coconut Grove.

Tiger was impressed with the Red House, but Boysie was more interested in the central police station opposite. "Boy, de most ignorant police in de world is de Trinidad police. Ah fuss dey stupid! Man, dey don't even know how to talk to people properly, dey like beast. But if yuh white, or if yuh have money, is all right. Ah know plenty people who does do all kind of scheme, but because dey have money de police don't do dem nutting. Is only poor people does catch dey arse."

They passed through the Red House and Tiger wanted to visit some of the rooms, but Boysie said what was the sense, hadn't he seen the Red House? So they went into Woodford Square. A tall Negro in a white gown was preaching to a crowd. He was drawing queer designs on the ground with a piece of chalk and predicting the ending of the world, warning the crowd to wash away their sins before it was too late. A few trees were covered with a kind of dry bean, and when the wind passed they rattled, and it sounded like waves cast up on a beach.

They sat down on a bench and Boysie pointed out Frederick Street and Tiger remembered he had to buy a bonnet for the baby.

"Dat is one ting yuh have to do for yuhself," Boysie told him, pushing out his legs and leaning back. "Sun too hot. Ah ain't going in no store wid yuh. Ah sitting down right here on dis bench in de shade, go and come back, Ah waiting for yuh."

The shopping centre of the city was crowded with week-end shoppers, Allied servicemen, and poor people looking in the show windows and feeling their pockets and purses. In five minutes, standing in one spot, Tiger could have seen representatives of all the races under the sun.

Tiger was a little afraid to venture into the store. He peeped in and saw so many people buying things. All the attendants appeared to be busy, he didn't know which one to approach. He saw a counter on which was displayed all manner of clothing for children. How was he to learn and have experience if he was such a coward? The people couldn't do him a damn thing. He had plenty money in his pocket, he was going to buy just as everybody else.

He went up to the counter where the attendant had a shapely backside turned. Tiger looked at it and said, "I want a bonnet for the baby."

The girl was sorting boxes on a shelf and didn't hear him. What she was doing wasn't necessary, but her department was surprisingly dull for a Saturday morning, and she was tired of just standing around. She was a good-looking Negro girl. Her father had Spanish blood; some of it flushed her face as she bent under the counter. She was thinking of a raffle in which she had invested two shillings. It was for a bicycle. If she could win! But it was just her luck to lose. It was going to be drawn at one o'clock when the stores closed, and the morning was dragging heavily. Whenever the horse-racing season was near, an Indian with a white beard used to come around selling sweepstake tickets, and she bought from him regularly. Every time she thought, This is it. Florida, New York, London, Paris. But she never won. Not even a consolation prize. Last Easter she had gone to Union, near San Fernando, for a meet. She had won five dollars in the pari. But she never gave up hope. One day she knew she would win. She used to rehearse in her mind just what she was going to tell the boss and her friends in the store. She wouldn't be too dramatic, although she could afford to be. She would just put her hands on her hips and look at him, from head to foot—no, that wouldn't do. She should deliberately do something wrong, and then when he began to talk to her she would show such *beautiful* indifference, like Bette Davis. She would smile and listen to him, and when he was through she would say, very calmly, without getting excited at all, "Mister, keep yuh blasted work!" And she imagined what a commotion that would cause —no, that wouldn't do. So she was always rehearsing how it would be when she won a sweepstake.

She glanced up at the store clock anxiously, then turned her back again.

Tiger looked at the backside and swallowed. He said, "I want a bonnet for the baby."

The girl turned and said, "Wait nar. Yuh is ah Russian? Yuh can't see I am busy doing something?"

Tiger fidgeted. The girl pushed the boxes in place, gave the new bicycle a quick look in her mind, and turned. "Now, wat it is you want?"

Before he could answer an elderly white woman came up. She had just told off an impudent policeman and was fuming. Imagine! He had had the impertinence to keep blowing her horn until she had to come out of the grocery where she had been ordering things for the week-end. Causing so much attention! And as usual a crowd of coloured idlers had stood around (it was amazing how quickly a crowd gathered in this city) while the policeman told her the car was parked too far out on the street, it was holding up the tram-car! "Look here, my good man, do you know who I am?" she had demanded in an icy tone. "Give me your number, I will speak to —— about you." True, he had backed down and apologized when she called ——'s name and said he was sorry, he didn't know, but damn it all, it was the impudence of the man! She would remember his number and speak to —— when she met him at the Country Club.

The attendant immediately leaned over the counter and a bright smile split the line of lipstick on her face. "Yes, madam, what I can do for you, please?"

Tiger said quietly, "I was here first."

The white woman sniffed the air and cast a surprised look at the Indian.

The attendant said sharply, "If yuh can't wait, go someway else!"

"I would like to get—" the woman began.

"But I was here first. My friend waiting up the road for me," Tiger explained, looking from one to the other.

The girl ignored him. The woman said, "Let me see what you have in cotton dresses, please. I want one for a girl of about seven years."

The attendant moved swiftly, piling boxes on the counter.

This thing shouldn't happen to him today, on his first trip to town. It was time he began to assert himself with those around him. "But look, is only fair that I get the bonnet first, you know," he said.

But he wavered. He wished Boysie were with him, he would have known what to do. He stood up helplessly, looking around and wondering if other people were noticing and laughing at him. He wanted to do the right thing, whatever it was.

But he couldn't understand the situation. What he wanted to do was to make a scene, demanding his rights. But instead he walked slowly out of the store.

Behind him the attendant said, "Ah sorry, madam, but yuh know how dese people rude. He look as if he just come from de country. Always pushing in front everybody else. This one suit yuh? Is a pretty colour."

The white woman brushed the incident from her mind as if she were flicking a speck off her dress. She just couldn't be bothered. Once was enough for the day. She paid for the dress and stood for a moment on the pavement before entering the car. The sun, almost overhead, struck her full in the face. She grimaced and cursed it under her breath. The country was beautiful, and life was far easier than in England, but it was so damn hot. She started the car and swung to one side to let a tram pass.

The girl slipped over to the haberdashery. "Girl, if Ah give yuh dis joke! A stupid coolie just come inside for a bonnet, and he playing he can't wait while I tending to Mrs. Cuthbert —you know, the white lady living in dat big house just opposite de cannonball tree in de savannah. If yuh see de man, like is the first time he come to town, a real country bookie!"

Her friend did as if she were sorting boxes of hairpins. "They too fast with theyself, girl, you didn't tell him wait? I know dem good, dey does have money wrap up in a cloth tie round they waist. Sometimes they examine everything yuh show dem, and in de end don't buy nothing! Yuh know the joke about the Indian man and the ham? Wait, just now I will tell yuh."

She dispatched a customer and returned. "One time an old Indian went in Canning's and ask to see ham. So Carl—Daisy's boy friend, nar—showed him one. He say it too small. So Carl bring ah bigger one. He still say it small. Well, Carl show him all de ham in the grocery, and still the coolie man ain't satisfy. So at last Carl, tinking de man want to buy bout twenty ham one time, bring the biggest one it had—a York ham—and tell him that is the best they have. The coolie lift it up, yuh know, and feel it good, and he say—yuh know what he say?— he say, 'Dis good one. Giveam twelve cents' worth!' "

"Ah never hear dat! Yuh should sent it to the *Guardian* West Indian humour contest and win one-twenty!"

"Yuh all right, if you tink I have time for dat. Things must be well dull by yuh, eh?"

"Yes, man, things dullish is a wonder, yuh know how Saturday does be busy."

"Girl, a master double showing at Empire dis evening. Yuh not going?"

"Wat they showing?"

"Robert Taylor in *Waterloo Bridge*, and *This Gun for Hire*. I don't miss Robert Taylor pictures at all, girl."

"Ah have a date this evening, man."

"Eh-heh! Yuh going in de gardens, eh?"

"Look, Mr. Benson coming, we go talk later."

Boysie said, "Yuh shoudda curse she modder. Why yuh didn't report she to de storewalker?"

"But why she treat me so, man? I was there first, before anybody else."

"Listen, is one ting yuh have to learn quick, and dat is dat wite people is God in dis country, boy. Was de same ting wen

I uses to work in de grocery. Was always wite people first. Black people like we don't stand ah chance."

"But, man, I ain't black. I is a Indian."

"Don't mind! As long as yuh ain't wite, dey does call yuh black, wedder yuh coolie or nigger or chinee. And too besides, yuh don't know dey have ah club way no black people cud go? Is a big-shot place. If yuh have money yuh stand ah chance; Ah know some black people who well get in because dey holding big. But if tomorrow come and yuh see dey aint have money, case, boy. Dey never to go back."

"But how everybody else does stand that kind of thing?"

Boysie rose from the bench and stretched. "Papa, is you who want to find out all dem tings. Ain't yuh want experience? Well, yuh getting it in yuh tail now."

One o'clock came and went, and the business places in Frederick Street exuded streams of employees, some dressed in warm jackets and with ties choking them under the blazing sun, the wiser ones with sleeves rolled up and necks open.

"Look, done all dis stupid talk," Boysie said suddenly, "Ah getting hungry. It have a restaurant in Queen Street way we cud get good *dhal pourri* and chicken curry, let we go."

"So now I can't get the bonnet," Tiger said as they ate.

Boysie belched and drank water. "Look, I going down St. James to see Stella. Wat yuh cud do, take a tram going to St. Clair, and go for a ride round de savannah. Ah ain't coming back till late, so don't worry to wait for me. Go by de stand in George Street and take bus or taxi and go home. Ah sure yuh can't get lose doing dat! Pay for de food and let we go."

Boysie saw Tiger on the tram and went to catch a trolley-bus himself.

It was like travelling in a train, he imagined. The bitterness had left him. The food was still warm in his belly, and now that he was on his own the trip became more adventurous. Anything could happen. If an incident like the one in the store recurred, he would know what to do. He wished something would happen, so he could show them. There were white people in the tram. He put his foot up on the seat in front, wanting the conductor to tell him to take it down. But when the conductor came for the fare he took no notice of Tiger's foot.

The tram was passing in the savannah, he could see boys kicking footballs and flying kites. And all the big houses where the white people lived. Such big houses! And pretty, with flower gardens in front, and vines growing on the walls. One day he would buy a house like that. Don't mind he was Indian. Don't mind he didn't have money now. He could be a big shot too, you won't say. In Chaguanas there was a rich Indian; he had a shop and a car and a big house. Not as big as these, but big still. When you have money, you could do anything.

The tram curved and travelled alongside Maraval Road. That must be the college Boysie was telling him to look out for. You could get knowledge in there. If his parents were rich, they might have sent him to school in Port of Spain, perhaps in that very same college. He would have grown up clever. He knew he would have learned all his lessons well and striven to be at the top of the class all the time. After, they might have sent him to study lawyer or doctor. Which one would he have chosen? It didn't matter, either one would have brought in plenty money, people were always going to court or getting sick. Moving among the big shots, he would have a car—a big one, new and shiny. This time so, see him visiting all the people in Barataria! Look, Mr. Tiger coming in he new car! He come back from England as a big lawyer, boy. He have plenty money, boy. "Good morning, Mr. Tiger! Good morning, chief!" He would stand them all drinks. Not because he was big shot he would ignore them. He would give a feast for the poor. He would have office in Port of Spain, and a secretary, like Mr. Rodriguez, the landowner in San Juan. This time so, the girls wild about him. He wouldn't let his father fix no marriage for him. He would pick the girl himself, and married in the church in the city, not in a bamboo tent! Hear the wedding bells ringing! See how many people come to Mr. Tiger wedding! So many cars, from Laventille to Port of Spain is only car, all of them going to the wedding. Man, after the wedding, people talk about it for weeks. It was talk of the town. Big picture in the *Guardian* papers, big headlines—Mr. Tiger, Prominent City Lawyer, Marries Doctor's Daughter. This time so, everybody know him for the smartest lawyer in town—it reach a time when he even have to refuse case! He have to expand the office, and now about three secretary working for him. As for the house he go be living in, jees and ages! If the Governor house have a hundred window, he own would have a hundred and a half. Which part you think that house going to be? Right in the middle of way all them white people living! You think he going to the Country Club every night, eh? But you wrong. Not because he have plenty money he go forget he own friends. He go be one big shot who the people go like, because he kind and helpful to the poor, every two, three week he giving feast for the poor. Jees and ages! That go be life! I tell you, hmm, if we had money, eh . . .

The tram curved, the wheels whined against the rails in the turning, and came to a halt in the Rock Gardens.

Tiger got out and walked around, looking at the flowers and the lilies in the two small ponds, his thoughts going round in circles, if this and if that. He walked across the road into the Botanical Gardens, up a lane lined with bay trees on which the bark peeled. And here and there people—strolling lovers hand in hand; a painter out in the open trying to get down a tree whose aspect was almost sensual; a young man deeply engrossed in a book, his back braced by the earth; an old woman sitting on a bench, a basket of sugar cakes by her side, gesticulating and mumbling to an invisible companion; a white woman with a dog on a leash, walking not enjoyably but for the exercise, in long strides, he saw the muscles of her calves flex with each step; a white man with a beard and a pipe and a camera; a group of American sailors being conducted on a tour of the gardens by a young Indian in a crumpled felt hat and dirty khaki pants and two teeth missing from his mouth. He stood up and heard the guide tell the Americans about a certain rare fruit which could rejuvenate the body, how old men came and begged him to get a few for them so they could satisfy their wives. He told the sailors that the only tree he knew of was one growing in the gardens, he would have shown them, but it was up on the hill and wasn't in fruit at that time of the year.

Tiger walked up the hill, where there was a flagpole. He watched down at most of the city—the savannah green and spreading, and all the houses where the white people lived, and the sea far out, loaded with ships, he could see the water shimmering under the glare of the sun. Looking down the coastline, he saw the Laventille swamp, its edge against the sea; he knew the swamp well, it extended inland right up to the back of the fields where he and the other farmers worked; boys used to set traps for crabs in the swamp. He looked up at the sky, where clouds shaped like the first forms of life sailed in the blue, going down west to pile up for the sunset later in the evening. He compared the broken-down hovels staining the Laventille hillside with the houses of the white people. Over there, nastiness and poverty, a tin cup of weak tea and a johnny cake or a roti. Over there, motorcars and—what did white people eat? Probably the best things, dishes he had never tasted in his life. He knew how every Sunday morning they came up to Barataria to buy the best beef and vegetables. Once he had heard Rita telling Urmilla about some kind of box in which they stored food, and it lasted for weeks. The box made ice cream and ice too. He would have to learn about all those inventions.

The wind came down from the hills behind St. Anns in thrusts of sweet, wild smells, and again he felt a power in it he would have liked to possess; he sat under a cashew tree and fell back on the grass, becoming aware of a hundred insect noises in the bush, the movement of leaf, and a throb in the earth itself, as if life buried there was pushing to come to the surface. It must be trees growing, it must be roots delving for food. He remembered the word "delving," the government agriculture man had used it in telling him about roots being the lifeline of plants. He felt as limitless as the space between him and the sky. Tiger didn't know the sky didn't exist except as a reflection: to him it was real, a blue bowl covering the world. Clouds were there because there had to be rain for things to grow; he knew which ones portended rainfall—not those white ones flying now, but great grey ones, tumbling into one another, until the whole sky was like slate. How high those clouds is? How high the sky? It must be good to fork up the land in the sky, it so blue! And everything you plant, it must be come out blue too. There would be books to tell him of all that, of course. He must hurry up and learn to read. He couldn't go around asking people questions all the time; he must have been a trouble to Boysie, that was why he paid so willingly for everything they drank and ate. When he was smaller, he never got answers. Why hadn't they sent him to school, instead of having him work away so many years in the canefields? He had learned nothing at all. It was only now he was learning. He remembered the man he had seen in the valley below, reading a book. He put himself in the place of the reader and turned a page. But that was all he could do. He could say it was a pretty book, or the pages were thick, or he might be able to count them all, one by one, but all the knowledge written down there—thousands and thousands of words, answering all his questions, and he could only stare. What sort of books would he read when he learned? Well, first it would be hard—you know, I can't read at all. I know the alphabet—when I was small we used to say a, b, c, in counting to see who would catch when we playing hoop. Like this—I know I can't explain good, but just suppose I could have talk good, so you could understand me? Like this:

A, b, c,
Mother catch a flea.
Flea die
Mother cry
One, two, three.

I know all, down to z, and I could count a little bit, man, you have to be able to count yes, or else people would give you wrong change in the shop! Well, first I would borrow them easy books from Henry. Is only a little time now he going to school, they must be easy, first primer and second primer. Is from them I will learn first. Then little bit, by degrees, I will learn to read the papers. Sookdeo does drink so much rum, man, I will have to buy plenty for him to teach me, but it worth it. After that, other books, about England and America and all them countries. But what I want to find out most is about things in general, about people, and how I does feel funny sometimes. Man, if I tell you bout things I want to find out! What I doing here now? Why I living? What all of we doing here? Why some people black and some white? How far it is from here to that cloud up there? What it have behind the sky? Why some people rich and some poor? But is what they fighting a war for? Man, I can't tell you about everything.

He imagined himself coming to the gardens to read; it was nice here, with the trees and flowers—look how much he was thinking now! A buttercup butterfly, bobbing about in the air, thrown off-course by the wind, righted itself and moved in graceful dips across his vision, and he watched it, holding his breath, hoping it would come to rest near him. But it settled on a leaf of the cashew tree only for an instant and took off in a hopping flight, falling down the hill. There wasn't very much he could look back on: it was 'the future he had to be concerned about.

He got up and looked at the sea again, feeling its deep movement. He would come back. As often as he could. It didn't cost much. Six cents on the bus, three cents on the tram, and he could be in another world. It was getting dark; he must have been in the gardens longer than he thought, for the sun was sinking. He watched it with deep feeling, not giving of himself so much as drawing from it what he could. It had lost its rays, and as he watched the salmon-coloured penny it seemed the horizon cut it in half and sent its blood spilling all over the sky. Deep purple merged in red and yellow, outlining the clouds. A flight of scarlet flamingoes from the mainland of Venezuela just made it and headed for the Laventille swamp. A blue evening haze settled on the hills. A twilight descended on the city. He had never paid much attention to the sunset before. Often he worked until it was dark, with his back to the west—it was easier to work in the evening when it was cool. But this one was different. It was for him the sun set. He was glad he was alone, Boysie would not have understood how he felt. He thought that when it rose in the morning things would change. For changes were sudden with him, one day he was a little boy and the next day he was a man; one day he didn't have to worry about anything and the next he had a wife and a child and the shop to pay. Something would happen.

"Aaye, man, yuh don't know six o'clock gone and is time to shut de gardens?" the Negro watchman shouted to him from the valley.

"All right, all right, I going now," and he ran down the hill.

CHAPTER SEVEN

A young Indian rode a bicycle carefully down ninth street, keeping as near as he could to the left edge where the road was less rough and rocky. When he got to Tall Boy's shop he dismounted and went inside, laying the bicycle in the grass. He bought a drink and asked Tall Boy's permission to put up a notice on the wall. Tall Boy said it was all right, as long as he didn't drive any six-inch nail in the wall and spoil it. The young Indian took a sheet of printed paper from his pocket and tacked it on the door where everybody who came into the shop could see it. Then he had another drink and rode away, to put up more notices near the main road.

Sookdeo entered the shop and saw Tall Boy staring at the notice. Sookdeo was a little out of breath; a Negro man had been teasing him and he had waved a stick wildly at him and shouted, "Come nar! One coolie killam one nigger today!"

Sookdeo sat down on a bag of rice and called for rum. But Tall Boy paid no attention. He was trying to read the notice on the door, he was a damn fool, he should have asked the man what it was about.

Sookdeo twisted his head and sent a lump of phlegm flying outside. He saw the notice and his head stayed turned and he read. The printing was plainly visible, but he got up and went closer, as if he wanted to make sure of what he read.

"Wat it is about, Sookdeo?" he asked as he went for the bottle of rum. He put a glass on the counter and poured a drink.

But Sookdeo didn't answer him. He gulped the drink and went out, running bow-leggedly, waving his arms and muttering to himself, forgetting his tools in the shop in his excitement. The sun threw his shadow long and grotesque before him, and he chased it to the gardens.

"Don't worry plantam any more ting!" he shouted to Tiger, using up the rest of his breath and almost gasping. "All of us have to leave de land!"

Tiger dropped his hoe and followed him. "What you mean? Explain yourself good, man." He held on to Sookdeo's arm.

"Everybody come dis side and hear dis!" Sookdeo shouted, standing up and breathing deeply. "Everybody come! Rajnauth, Sampath, Deen, Boysie, all come! Big ting happening! We have to leave de land!"

The farmers grouped about him, wiping their faces in their shirts, and Boysie said, "Wat yuh mean? Way yuh get dat news from?"

Sookdeo began talking to himself. "Is nearly twenty year I dis side Barataria, and nutting ever happen. Life going good. Now, is trouble. Everybody moveam. Wat we go do? Which part we go go?"

"Look, man, where you get this news from?" Tiger asserted himself and shook Sookdeo by the shoulders.

"In Tall Boy shop!" Sookdeo became excited again and trembled. "Ah big notice up dat side! All coolie clear out of garden, American coming to build road here."

"Ah don't understand dis man at all," Deen said. "He must be drunk. Let we go by de shop and read dis notice weself."

They walked together, afraid to take Sookdeo seriously,

wanting to believe it was all a joke, that the old man was
making fun with them. But before they reached the shop Tiger
knew something big was going to happen. He could smell it
in the wind, feel it in the sun.

When they got to the shop villagers were already crowding
around the notice, talking excitedly. Rita, a parcel of flour
in her hand, was telling them, "Good ting my husband have
a work in de base. Is all dem Indian who have garden down
de road who in trouble." She saw Tiger and told him, "Yuh
learn to read in good time! Read wat dat notice say!"

The crowd quieted down, giving those whom the notice
concerned a chance to read. "Yuh playing scholar, Tiger,"
Deen said. "Ah don't understand good, and all ah we can't
see de notice good. Explain it to we, nar?"

Tiger read slowly to himself, taking his time over the big
words, his lips moving soundlessly. It was something real big
that was going to happen, like the wedding and the thing and
the baby.

He cleared his throat. "Well, as you could see for yourself,
the Americans and them going to build a road right by here.
The notice from the estate people. It say that we will have to
quit our garden, as is right there the road will be passing. It
say that we will be com-pen-sated by the estate company. I
don't know what that word mean, but the sense is that we will
get money for whatever we lose. It say we have two weeks
to clear out. It say a man will come from the estate-owner
office, and ass-ess the gardens and them. That must be mean
to see how much crop we have plant. And we will get com-
pen-sat-ion to match. It say that we could get all the informa-
tion from the office in San Juan. Then below here like they
add something, let me see good. Oh yes, they say that the
road will not take up all the room, that maybe some people
will have to move and others could stay. And it say that who-

ever still want to keep garden could get other land to rent, just as soon as the Americans finishing surveying the land to see how much they will want. But it say again that the best thing to do is to see the man in the San Juan office, who will explain properly."

"Ah-ah! Tiger, yuh garden dey first, is sure yuh go have to move!"

"But is a helluva ting happening, *oui!*"

"Sookdeo might get away, as he garden back, near de swamp."

"So wat we going to do? Ah still don't understand dis business good."

It looked like nobody was going to work again for the rest of the morning. Sookdeo was already having his third drink, and others were calling for more glasses, with plenty ice.

Rita, her hand loosely on her hip, listened to them arguing.

"Is none ah my business," she said, addressing Tiger in particular, "but allyuh too damn foolish. Why one ah yuh don't go San Juan and find out wat dis ting is all about, and den decide wat allyuh go do?"

"That is a good idea, Rita," Tiger agreed, then turned to the rest. "What all you say?"

"Well, you go nar, Tiger," Rajnauth urged. "Go and find out everything, and come back and tell we."

Deen said, "Tiger is ah damn fool. Yuh better let somebody else go, somebody who responsible and could talk like man for we."

Tiger wasn't hurt. He felt calm, because he had known something big was going to happen. This thing was affecting him personally. He said, "I don't care what all you do, but I know I going to find out for myself. I ain't going to let nothing happen to me again and I don't know why it happen."

"Yuh right boy, Tiger, yuh right," Boysie put in, "but is no sense all ah we going. One man cud go and find out for everybody. You go nar, and wen yuh come back pass round by me and give me de lowdown. If Ah ain't home, meet me by de garden."

"Well, is to go right now," Tiger said, "no use waiting. I just running home to change my clothes."

Tall Boy leaned over the counter. "All right! All right! All who ain't buying cud go home and stop jamming up de shop!"

"Half-pound saltfish!"

"Two pound ah flour!"

"Ah leave me pot on de fire, Tall Boy, don't mind dese people, just give me half-bottle cooking oil quick, and mark it."

"You come over by de bar, man, and let Mary sell in de shop. We want some cold soda—how yuh cutting de ice so small?"

Some went away, talking and arguing, wondering what was going to happen when the Americans came. Notices had been put up by the main road and in all the shops in the village, and everybody knew what was happening. Those who were not directly affected by the notice joked at the others, telling them they would have to take in washing and keep livestock.

Tiger told Urmilla, "Something big happening. Ask Rita, she go tell you about it," and he ran out and caught a bus on the main road.

It was about three o'clock when he came back, perspiring in the torrid afternoon heat. It was only then that he ate his lunch, telling Urmilla that the next day American surveyors were coming to mark off the course the road would take.

Boysie wasn't at home—Tiger found him in the shop with Sookdeo. Boysie was drunk. He was telling Sookdeo that he could outdrink him any day, and that was a sure sign. The rest of the men had gone back to the comfort and security of their gardens to work as if nothing had happened, but the morning's news was on every lip. It was all they talked about, hoeing and cutlassing halfheartedly.

The girls and the women got together in the shade.

"Girl, how yuh would like to sleep wid ah Yankee man?"

"Ha ha, yuh better don't let Rajnauth hear yuh, he go cut off yuh head wid de cutlass!"

"Ah hear dey does have money like fire, and good cigarette. Ah hear Rita say how dey nice, dat dem girls in Port ah Spain going wild over dem."

That night Tiger sat on a cushioned chair in Joe Martin's drawing room and talked.

"This is a big thing going to happen, Joe."

"Man, keep quiet. Everyting dat happen, yuh does say is ah big ting."

"But you don't understand, Joe, I might have to move my garden. Suppose I don't get enough money? I ain't have so much thing plant, I was waiting for the rainy season to start. The more things you have plant, the more com-pen-sat-ion you get."

"Don't worry yuh head. If de worse come to de worse, yuh cud always get ah work wid de Yankees. Dey sure to take local labour to help build de road."

Tiger sat up excitedly. "But you know I didn't think of that! I could get a job with them for truth! Work for plenty money like you, to hell with the garden! But, Joe, you know that is a good idea, boy? How much you getting down at the base now?"

"Take it easy, pardner, yuh won't get as much money as you tink."

"But still, man, it go be plenty! I could save up! Buy house like you!"

Joe laughed loudly. "Rita, yuh listening to him? He want to buy house now!"

"Well, is what you think, Joe? You think I want to live in a mud hut all the days of my life?"

"Ah lot of allyuh Indian people like dey satisfy wid dat."

"That is them, but I have ambition, Joe. I take my own time, and learn to read and write little bit. I wasn't shame when I borrow first primer book from Henry to learn from. Every night I learn a little bit. More and more. I could read as good as Sookdeo now."

"But, Tiger, tell me someting. Yuh tink dat because yuh cud read and write yuh is ah better man dan me?"

"Is not a matter of who better than who, Joe. Is just me, inside of me. Things I want to learn, things I want to find out. Boy, life was different with you, yes. You grow up in the city, you had a lot of experience. If even you not have education, you still not a fool. But look at me. A stupid coolie boy from the country, can't even read and write. That is what people does say about me. They does call me a force-ripe man. You think I like to remain ignorant? You think I don't want to find out what happening England and America? Ah, boy, plenty things change since I come Barataria to live. Yes. People used to laugh and call me a little boy. When I go to town, they ignoring me as if I don't exist. The first time, I used to think as long as you have wife and child, you is a man. So long as you drink rum and smoke, you is a man. That is what my father and them tell me. But no. It take more than that. Look at you, you is a man. People does treat you like a man, show you respect."

"Yuh too chu-chut, yuh see. People does bully yuh, and do yuh as dey like."

"That was long time, boy. Nobody ain't going to play as if

they better than me from now on. I getting experience, I learning. Just now I going to read big books."

"Is experience dat go teach yuh, not books."

"But still, men does write down their experience in books, and you could learn from them. Joe, you making joke, man. I bet you with all your experience it have some things that you don't know."

"Like wat so? Look, yuh want ah cigarette?"

Tiger took one, and Joe gave him a light and tossed the matchstick on the floor. Tiger inhaled strongly and exhaled, pushing out his underlip and guiding the smoke upwards across his eyes and forehead. He spat out a piece of tobacco and went on, "Who make you? What you doing here now? What all of we doing here?"

"Ah don't understand yuh. Dat is ah stupid question. Yuh talking, and I sitting down here in de chair listening to yuh. Rita and Henry someway inside, and yuh wife must be sleeping. Oder people must be minding oder people business, as usual. Some gone theatre, some loafing about town, some sleeping—"

"Is not so I mean, man, and you well know. I mean it in a different way, like how everybody in the world come, and why they living. Like that."

Joe laughed again. "Why yuh want to find out dat?"

Tiger looked surprised. "But you don't want to find out too? You don't want to know why you living, and other people, and why it have a sun, and why trees does grow, and how people does live in America and England, and how—"

"Hold a key, hold a key," Joe said. "Now listen to me, pardner. All ah dat dat yuh want to find out is ah set ah balls. Dat only for minister and teacher and mad people. Why yuh tink dat knowledge go help yuh? Boy, listen. It had a time when I did small, dey send me to school in Nelson Street. All right.

I learn abc and how to count. By de time dey ready to put me in first standard, I decide long time it ain't have no future in dat. I used to break *buisse*—yuh know wat dat is?"

Tiger shook his head sadly. "I never went to school."

"Well, like yuh never had boy days! Wen yuh break *buisse* is wen yuh run away from school and go dancing top or pitching marble or tiefing mango in people garden, or going down by de sea to bade. Regular, I uses to break *buisse*. De teacher didn't even know me good; wen he see me face in school he used to say, 'Who is dat new pupil?' All right den. Ah grow up big, having experience. Ah screw so much woman dat I can't even remember dem. Ah tief. Ah go hungry. Ah drink rum. Ah smoke. Ah play cards—Ah was a rummy test in me days, and don't talk bout wappee! Yuh cud play cards?"

"No."

"Well, look at dat! If yuh cud ah play, all now so we cud be playing some steel rummy instead of talking balls. Anyway, all kind ah ting happen to me. So ah get a job wid de Yankee. Ah meet Rita. She say, 'Boy, ah like yuh, le' we go and live together.' Dat was de case. Is so yuh see me here today. Me belly full. Ah have a house to live in. Ah have ah wife, and don't mind Henry ain't my child, is just as if he belong to me. If yuh look sharp, Ah save up money and buy ah car! But wat I go do wid car? Ah don't want to be no millionaire, Ah have enough money. But Ah still living good, and Ah does have some happy times wid my friends. So wat happen now?"

Joe flicked cigarette ash on the floor, and Tiger opened a matchbox and tapped his in. "You mean to say, Joe, that you never had ambition to go to college or get a good office job?"

"But why, papa? Ah man cud live happy without all dem tings."

"Well, Joe, that is you, but as for me, I can't be happy until

I find out things. I suppose is just that we different from one another. Everybody can't be the same."

"Well, Ah agree wid yuh dere. But at de same time, tell me someting. Is how yuh expect to be dis big scholar? Yuh forget de wife and de baby. If yuh start to make money, is dem yuh have to tink of first."

"That all right, don't worry. First thing is to make the money, then afterwards I could bother bout that."

Tiger left Joe and walked outside in the street. Tonight was a big night. It was like the time Chandra was born. The moon was full, lighting up the village. Trees cast shadows. A late goods train rumbled and belched black smoke. It slowed as it travelled through the village, then surged on, and he could hear the grinding sound of the wheels grow fainter. He just felt like walking and letting the night wind hit him in the face. Boysie and some other young men were sitting on a concrete culvert in sixth street, trading smutty jokes; he didn't feel like it tonight. On the opposite side three Negroes were beating softly on steel-band instruments.

He walked out to the main road and bought a roasted corn from a woman vendor. She was fanning the coal-pot and turning the corns on the hot coals. She charged him six cents and he knew it was too much, there were good corn crops in the village, he was having some difficulty in getting a fair price for his. But he didn't argue. He munched the corn and walked down the main road, towards tenth avenue. The sky was like velvet, the moon's glow dimmed the twinkle of stars. Vehicles roared and sped up and down. A prostitute approached him with an unlighted cigarette but changed her mind as she came closer and turned away. He thought, It must be a hard night for she if she can't find a sailor or a soldier, and so much of them all about! He could have shown her money, and that would have brought her back. But what was the use? It didn't prove you were a man. Nor drinking rum, nor swearing, nor screwing a woman. The way Joe talked, you would think these things counted. But look at Joe, man! He still young, and yet he have no ambition! What sort of man is that?

He swung into tenth avenue and went into the fields. He remembered the night he had come, when the baby was born. It was plenty different then. He sat down in his garden, and then, just to see if the same emotions would overcome him, lay full length on the grass, and watched up at the sky. He was smiling to himself. It seemed such a long time ago. But he was a boy then. Now he was—what? A man? Maybe, but not a man like Joe Martin or Boysie or any of the others. They were content, he was not. He remembered how he had planned to sell his first harvest for knowledge, to an unknown power. What a waste of tomatoes and ochroes and lettuce that would have been. For he knew now how to go about searching for knowledge. And the power—why, the power was all around him, he could feel it throbbing in the earth, humming in the air, riding the night wind, stealing through the swamp. The power was free, all you had to do was breathe it in, deep and full, until your chest felt like bursting. And glory in it—in the depth of the night, in the rustling trees, in the immense space between earth and sky. Sometimes, like now, I does think about if they have a God. But if even they have, you don't have to do anything special. You just have to live a clean life. Don't hurt nobody. You could do just as you please, only—well, you must have some sort of respect, like realize how small you is, and how big the sky is. And—well, sort of have a respect, man, for what sending the rain and what making the sun shine. That is all. It not so hard to do. God is a good man, don't mind He didn't send a boy child when I did ask Him. He must be know why people fighting war and killing up one another! He must be know everything. Is funny how sometimes I does think of

God, and I don't even know Him! And then it have times when I don't think of Him at all. But I sure He ain't mind, man. You think is always I does have time to think of He?

He heard a sound. He wasn't sure what it was. He propped an elbow and raised himself. It sounded like a crab digging a hole. He looked round but saw nothing, although the light of the moon was full on the fields. The sound continued, and he got up. Someone was working over there, in Sookdeo's plot of land. Who could it be? No man worked in his garden in the night. He saw a figure and went up to it bravely.

"A-a, Sookdeo, is you! You frighten me, man! Is what you doing in the garden so late in the night?"

Sookdeo turned around sharply, dropping his cutlass. He scooped it up again and demanded, "Who dat dere? Who dat?"

"Is Tiger. You don't recognize me?"

"Wat yuh doam here now, eh? Yuh spying on Sookdeo, eh?"

"No, man. I just taking a walk, and I hear noise, so I come to see what it is."

Sookdeo relaxed. He was perspiring, his face reflected moonlight. He had had his last drink at seven o'clock, just before Tall Boy closed the shop. And after he had gone home and eaten, he remembered about the notice to quit the land, and what it said about compensation.

"Listen, boy," he said, and his body shook, as it always did when he was sober, "yuh is de first man see Sookdeo dis side garden in de night. Yuh wondering why Ah here! Because is moonlight. Ah will tellam one secret, because yuh want to learn tings. If yuh wantam crops to come good, must plant when moon full!"

Tiger stared at him. Sookdeo laughed dryly.

"Yuh don't believe? Is how yuh tink my crops grow big and

strong quick? Because Ah does always plant in full moon. Dat is why yuh never seeam Sookdeo working hard daytime."

"If even is true, is a late secret. You forget about the Americans building road. Everybody might have to leave they garden."

"Yuh tink Sookdeo chupid, eh? Yuh saying to yuhself, 'Look at de old man, he so foolish, he still planting ting and next two week all de gardens going!' Dat is wat yuh saying, eh? But Sookdeo ain't no fool, boy. Yuh forget bout de compensation?"

"No."

"Yuh forget how it say, 'How much crop yuh haveam, so much yuh get pay.' Yuh forget dat?"

"No, I not forget."

"Well den, leave me alone. Wat time dat estate man come dis side and he ask Sookdeo, 'Sookdeo, how much crop yuh haveam?' Sookdeo say, 'Chief, me haveam plenty crop plant.' And me showam."

"But, Sookdeo, that man coming in a week. You think what you plant now will have time to grow?"

"Must grow, boy. Full moon dat side"—he pointed to the sky —"and Sookdeo dis side. Must grow!"

"I don't think the full moon have anything to do with it."

"A-ha! Yuh don't know sense, dat's why. Ah tell yuh, if yuh plant tings wen de moon full, it bound to grow quick." He looked closely at Tiger. "Yuh not haveam ah flask in back pocket? Ah too tirsty, man. Ah cud do wid a drink. Look how me hand shakeam, is only rum him want to keep him quiet."

"All the time you go drink so, man, even in the night? Wait until morning. If even I had, I wouldn't give you. But tell me, Sookdeo, why you does really drink so much rum?"

Sookdeo bent his knees and dropped down on a bank.

"Yuh still small, boy. Wen yuh get big man like me, wen yuh

go trough wat I go trough, yuh will drink rum too. Listen,
Ah will tell yuh someting. Don't tellam nobody! Right now,
Ah too frighten."

Tiger sat down next to him. "How you mean frighten?"

"Yuh can't see? Not haveam eye? Look how old I gettam.
Weak. Hand, foot, head hurt in de night. Now, we have to
leave garden side. Wat me go do? Which part I go? Boy, Ah
frighten too bad. It have a time wen it ain't have no rum for me
to drink, and I start to tink. Ah tink, 'Sookdeo, is wat yuh do
wid yuh life at all? Is wat going to happen to yuh? Who go
bury you wen yuh dead?' Boy, time like now so, wen no rum
to drink, I does want to dead. Yuh don't know, boy. Since I
come Trinidad side, ah little boy. Work in canefield. Grow big
man. Nutting boy, nutting. Old carat hut, leaking. Garden
which side Barataria. Plenty rum. Ah does see young girls and
like dem, but Ah too old! Ah get old before me time! No more
life in me. Nutting, boy, nutting. Don't let dat happen your
side, boy. Yuh right. Don't mind everybody laugh at yuh.
Everybody say, 'But look at Tiger, nar! He playing scholar!
He learning to read and write!' But yuh right. Yuh want to
come man like me? Go in de city, don't stay dis side. Get ah
work wid wite people in office. If yuh stay here, wat? Digging
hole in ground. Rainy season come. Tomatoes come. Sell, buy
rum. Go back in garden again. Sun burning yuh! Every day,
same ting dis side. Ah frighten, boy. Ah never had boy child,
only girl, dem is trouble self. If Ah had ah boy, he wud be big
like yuh now. But if anyting, he driving taxi! Plenty Indian
driving taxi, have big car, making plenty money. Boy, you
young. Go way from here. Yuh don't know, boy. If yuh stay
dis side, and get like Sookdeo, everybody laugh at yuh."

Tiger said uncertainly, "No need to worry, Sookdeo. If you
lose you garden we might get work with the Americans and
them, helping to build the road."

"Who, me? Ah so old Ah can't do hard work like wen Ah did young. American won't want Sookdeo."

"But I sure it will have plenty work in building that road. Is not only young men will get work. Girls and women too, and you could do something. Sookdeo, tell me something—you believe it have a God?"

"But how? You fadder and modder never tell yuh bout dat?"

"Well, is a funny thing, but when I did small I never used to pay attention to all the ceremonies and meetings and prayers they have. I know it had a time when a wite minister used to come, and preach in the village, and he tell we it have a God, and he tell we about a man named Jees, or something so. He say how when everybody dead, if they live good life, they go in a nice country behind the sky, which part milk and honey does flow in the rivers! He say we must pray to this God and ask Him to help, but plenty time we pray, and nothing happen. Plenty people turn into Christian though."

Sookdeo said, "Well, how? Don't know Indian people haveam own God? Don't know bout Bhagwan? To pray Kali for rain wen dry season too long? Yuh growam chupid or wat?"

"Man, I tell you, I never used to pay attention to all of that."

"Yuh don't know right dis side we haveam meeting, play drum, sing Indian song, right by ninth street corner? Don't know one Roodal dat side, teacham Hindi?"

"I never grow up in too much Indian custom. All different kinds of people in Trinidad, you have to mix up with all of them."

"Well, Ah don't know bout dat. So wat God yuh prayam to?"

Tiger watched the moon. "I don't know. But whenever big things happen, I does go out and look all about, at the hills, and the trees, and the sky, and them. And I does get a funny feeling, as if strength coming inside me. That must be God."

"Ah don't likeam dis kind talk."

"But why you fraid, Sookdeo? How you mean fraid?"

"Ah just tell yuh. I old man. Ah fraid wen new tings happen."

"You must have to believe in something! You must have to have something you does pray to! Look at me, I can't explain, but I does feel a power in the space all about. You don't feel anything now? Look at the moon and them stars and up on the hills. You don't think it have somebody who make them, somebody who is a big man like a God?"

"Ah tell yuh me don't likeam dis talk. Leave me alone to plant me seeds." Sookdeo got up and began digging holes in a line, working fast, muttering to himself, as if he had completely forgotten Tiger.

A white cloud, pushed by a swift wind, moved under the moon and cast a brief shadow. Tiger walked away without another word.

And Sookdeo, mindful of the compensation and fearful of the future, planted his seeds.

The weather changed with tropical suddenness next day. The morning dawned cloudy, with a slight drizzle. Men went to work just as if nothing had happened. Towards midmorning the sun burst out of the clouds, by noon it was overhead with a burning heat, and at one o'clock a jeep was in San Juan in front of the estate office.

Everyone was waiting for the Americans to come and measure out the land. Tiger had a premonition his garden would go. He wanted it to go, he wanted things to be different. If even the road was going to be built away from his garden, he had no intention of continuing to farm the land; he was going to give it up and work with the Americans. Sookdeo was drunk and didn't care what happened. Tiger was surprised to see how care and the fearful look on his face of the night before vanished with a few drinks. All the others wanted the matter to be settled as quickly as possible so they could know how they stood. The women talked about the Americans; one or two who had had experience with them in the city made confessions, and they laughed and giggled, and all longed to sleep with Americans too and have something exciting to talk about.

The jeep drove into sixth avenue from the main road. Bunsee, the Indian man from the office, sat in the back with two officers. Two soldiers were in front. Bunsee had on a new suit and a panama hat. It was the first time he had ever been on so important a job. He felt the importance and showed it. He smoked a Lucky Strike cigarette which one of the officers had given him, and he leaned back in the jeep and surveyed what he could see of the village. He wanted the Indian people especially to see him sitting back there, at home with two big white men. That is why he had suggested that they drive down sixth avenue—they could have gone down the main road and entered the far end of the village. And when the people stared his chest swelled. A Negro woman pushing a box cart, buying empty bottles, stopped and put her hands on her hips and said, "*Eh bien, oui!* But look at de coolie man, nar!" Vendors whispered among themselves that the Americans had come; one of them hailed, "Good morning, Mr. Bunsee!"—though it was afternoon—and Bunsee turned his head slightly and frowned. He didn't want the officers to think he was friendly with these people dressed in torn clothing selling vegetables by the roadside. They had their place and use, like when they brought him the best of their produce, seeking favours. "Mr. Bunsee, yuh is ah big shot. Yuh cud speak to Mr. Rodriguez for me, ask him please to extend de lease, tings really hard, de dry season make all de crops poor, and Ah can't pay de land rent." Or there was a wedding in the village, and he would be asked, and given a front seat, and the best to eat. He was godfather for nearly a dozen of the village children. When a child was born it was, "Mr. Bunsee, yuh go be de godfadder of dis chile, please?" A godfather was supposed to assist in the bringing up of the child, buy shoes and clothing and schoolbooks if the parents were too poor. Why the hell did they keep asking him? He had never done anything for any of the children, and they knew it, yet they still came to him, because he was a big shot, because he was working for Mr. Rodriguez. They were proud to say, "Yuh know who is godfadder for dis chile? Is Mr. Bunsee, yes!" Like the Indians in Port of Spain, he was completely Westernized and tolerated their ceremonies and feasts with a faint amusement. Perhaps after this job of assessing the gardens he would get a rise and move into the city. He would speak to Mr. Rodriguez about it. He was in love with a Portuguese-Indian girl who lived in Laventille. Like him, she was very modern; it was a joke with them when they talked about marrying. She would say, "Look, Carl, we ain't getting married under bamboo, you know! No Indian wedding for we in no tent! Is de Roman Catholic church in Port of Spain!" That was the snag, because he would have to leave his own religion and become a Roman Catholic if he wanted to marry her. It was always a quarrel with his mother and father, who were staunch Hindus and disliked the girl, saying she was the cause of him forgetting the habits and customs of his own people. They didn't want the marriage at all, but when they said they wanted him to be happy he pressed on that point and said he would be happy only if he married her. He would have done it regardless of what they said, but they were wealthy; his father had a shop and a big house in San Juan, and he was hoping for the gift of a house from him as a wedding present. So he argued and pleaded, and they were breaking down; if he could only get a rise from Mr. Rodriguez—he would tell him he was going to marry—everything would go all right.

The jeep bumped into ninth street and one of the officers said, "Holy smoke! These roads are like hell!"

Bunsee hastened to explain, plans were under way for all the streets in the village to be asphalted, but there were great difficulties, the estate was fully aware of the deplorable (he deliberately used this word, which he had read in the *Trinidad Guardian* when someone in Barataria wrote a letter to the editor complaining about the streets) conditions, but soon they would get to work.

"Queer village," one officer mused to the other. "There's a thatched hut, and next to it a small modern bungalow. And look at the different kinds of people in the streets!"

The driver cursed softly as the front wheel struck a rock and threw the jeep to one side; he let go the steering wheel and the car came back on the road.

"Take it easy, Smithy," the other soldier said.

The jeep pulled up where ninth street met tenth avenue, and though Bunsee was sitting at the end he pulled in his knees awkwardly to allow the officers to get out before him.

"Good morning, Mr. Bunsee!" "Morning, chief!"

Bunsee waved his hand to the group of villagers. They stood there as if they expected him to make a speech or something.

He called out to Sookdeo, "You is the oldest man, not so? Come and show us the way!"

But there was no way to show: the tracks on the thin strip of land between the village and the swamp were plainly visible. The Americans took surveying instruments from the jeep and went into the fields, and Bunsee knew he had made a fool of himself in front of the officers, wanting to show off to the villagers. Even Sookdeo said, "Road right dere, don't seeam?"

Tiger nudged Boysie and the two of them laughed; the others shuffled and held their mirth back. Bunsee turned his back on them and walked quickly to meet the Americans.

When he was out of earshot they all started to laugh, and Sookdeo imitated Bunsee, and Boysie explained to Tiger how to distinguish a private from a corporal and a sergeant. None of them really felt like working. Since yesterday there had been a lull; they just came down to the gardens to see what the Americans would do and whether the estate man would tell them anything.

The surveying party was out of sight. Tiger wanted to see what they were doing, and he and Boysie left the others. The officers were looking through something like a spying glass and pointing down the fields, far away, to where clumps of bamboo grew behind the village.

And as he pointed Tiger followed the direction and imagined the road winding through the fields, a long, pretty road, not like those stupid roads in Barataria where you "stumped" your toe all the time, but a real road, built by the Americans. Boysie had said that when the Americans built anything, it was worth looking at. And Joe had told him how they had laid out the base at Chaguaramas, the big buildings, the well-paved streets. How different the land would be! Now it was just the swamp over there, where the boys went to hunt and catch crabs. And here, the bush and the gardens. And over there, the village. The road would pass between the swamp and the village. Cars, trucks, all sorts of vehicles running on the land he was standing on now, where tomatoes and lettuce and pigeon peas and corn grew! The road curving into the shade of the bamboo, going far away, behind San Juan, behind St. Joseph, all up by Tacarigua, until it reach the American base! The road he would help to build. Don't mind Joe! Is really something big! Afterwards, when everything finish, I could look and say, "Tiger help to build that road. Look at all them cars and jeeps and trucks passing. You see there, right by where that jeep slowing down now? I remember, when we was building the road, it had a tree right there, it so hard to come out we had to use dynamite and blow it up, and—"

"Boysie," he said softly, "you could see the road?"

"Which road yuh talking bout?"

"The one we going to build. You can't see it? Look how the officer pointing. You see it coming down here, right by where we standing up watching them, then down there, through your garden, through the fields, pass where Deen have rice plant, by the ending down there, right through the bamboo. A pretty road, boy. Better than what they make down in the base. Better than the main road. It smooth like velvet. It wide—four, five car could pass one time. You can't see it, Boysie? You really can't see it?"

"Man, stop making joke, nar!" Boysie said.

"You have no imagination," Tiger said. "I could see it, though, as if it was here already."

They could see Bunsee with a map of the district in his hands, and the Americans looking over his shoulders as he pointed out certain landmarks. Tiger wanted to go nearer, but Boysie said they could see everything from where they were. The soldiers drove pickets in the ground, and the officers talked to Bunsee, sweeping their hands over the area. They could see Bunsee nodding his head, agreeing to everything they said.

After about half an hour the party returned to the jeep. Sookdeo was entertaining the villagers by sitting behind the wheel in the jeep and showing them how to drive it. He leaped out with surprising agility when he saw the Americans approaching and lost himself quickly among the people in the back of the crowd.

Bunsee addressed them. "Who plot of land is that by de mango tree?"

"Mine, chief, mine!" Sookdeo came to the front.

"Well, I think that is the onlyest garden that could stay. But everything not finish, you understand that? We only make a short survey. You will know all details later on in the week."

Tiger wasn't listening to Bunsee. He was looking at one of the officers who had a kind, tired face. He was making up his mind to talk to the officer. He worked himself up, swallowing hard. It was only one thing he wanted to find out. They couldn't do him a damn thing for asking a question.

He moved out of the group and addressed the officer.

"Mr. Officer, when you all start to build the road, I could get a job with you all, helping?"

The officer, already seated in the jeep, laughed. "Well son, I don't know about that. I won't be here, for one thing. But we would be employing civilians, wouldn't we, Frank?"

The other officer said, "Sure, there'll be plenty jobs."

"Thank you, mister," Tiger said.

The others looked as if he had done a startling thing, but he said to hell with them in his mind, because he had spoken to the officer, and got a reply, and nothing had happened. Only Bunsee was looking at him as if he had committed a crime. Boysie whispered, "But yuh brave, man!" And Tiger shrugged his shoulders.

Next morning the young Indian who had put up the notice came back to Barataria. He dismounted in front of Tiger's hut.

"Aaye, boy," he called out to Tiger milking the cow under the rose mango tree, "your name Tiger?"

Tiger went up to him. "Who you calling 'boy'? You don't see I is a big man?"

The estate clerk handed him a form without replying. He asked, "Where Rajnauth living?"

"In tenth street."

"And which part Boysie living?"

"By Tall Boy shop."

"And Deen?"

"You think I is a postman or what? I don't know, man. You might find all of them by the shop."

He went inside and showed Urmilla the form. "You see, is the same thing I tell you. My garden is one that have to go. But I will get a big job with the Americans and work for plenty money."

Later he met Sookdeo in the shop and said, "You see, you didn't get any form. You could stay, Sookdeo, and keep you garden still! You don't have to move!"

"Ah too glad, boy," and the old man couldn't hide his relief. He sang an Indian song and offered Tiger a drink.

Before they drank Tiger said, "Sookdeo, I never thank you for helping to learn me to read, but you know I grateful. If wasn't for you to help me, now so I still learning in first primer book!" He took the newspaper off the counter. "Now I could read for you!"

"See if no news dat side bout American building road?"

Tiger glanced down the columns on the front page. "But yes," he cried. "Look something here bout it, man!"

"Read it nar, see wat it say."

"It say—" He stopped. He read the news quickly and threw the paper to one side. "It don't say anything new, man. Is just what we know already."

The rest of the week passed by quietly. The gardeners did odd jobs about their huts. Only Tiger went to the fields every morning. He wanted to impress the landscape on his mind,

how the trees grew, how the drains near the ricefields ran,
how each man had planted. Because he knew it would all
change, and he wanted to be able to remember how it was at
first, before the road was built. He went into every garden.
He noticed that the seeds Sookdeo had planted had sprouted;
he smiled to himself. If rain fell over the week-end, by the time
Bunsee came they would be about six inches high. Deen didn't
keep a clean garden, all that black sagebush should have been
cut down. And those banks should have been higher in the
ricefield. He didn't care about his own garden; if even he didn't
get any compensation it would be all right. Just as long as he
got a job to help build the road.

And when he went home he thought about it, and he told
Urmilla, "You know what. I will write down everything what
happen. How we had garden, and how the Americans come,
and how we had to leave, and how they build the road—"

"Don't talk so loud, Tiger, you go wake up the baby."

"To hell with the baby! I talking bout the future, and how
we will build a big house to live in."

"You don't care for the child again. Ever since you learning
to read and to write, you having big ideas, you going to town,
you like you don't care to stay home again, like you don't care
about anything."

He used to lay there, staring at the carat roof, and remem-
bering his life. What Sookdeo had told him. What if things
went somehow wrong, if he got to be an old man like Sookdeo,
with a wife and a girl child, and an awful fear inside, the fear of
having nothing in front or behind? He imagined the children
in the village teasing him: "Tiger! Tiger, yuh old drunkard!"
But he told himself fiercely that things just had to turn out
right. In his sleep he tossed and groaned and ground his teeth,
and Urmilla was afraid for the child.

A kind of gloom settled on the village, seen and felt even in the brilliancy of the sun and the constancy of the wind. It was like a waste of sunny, seed-bursting days, for no one bothered now with farming the land, just waiting around for Mr. Bunsee to come and assess. Those who had livestock grazed the animals in the savannah. Deen investigated the possibilities of selling chickens and measured out the space of land at the back of his hut for putting up a fowl-run. If they had to turn from the land the only thing to do was to raise livestock. Everybody checked up on how many hens and cocks they had; Tall Boy sold more chicken mash in that week than he had ever sold before. Even the middle-class people who worked in Port of Spain observed that the farmers were not behaving as usual; when Urmilla made the rounds selling milk they asked her about it, and she said they were just waiting to see what would happen.

Bunsee came on the Tuesday morning, early, and the farmers went with him and counted their crops. He had a copybook and a pencil, and he marked down their names and told them offhand how much money he thought they would get, but everything had to be checked at the office. Only Boysie and Tiger refrained from leasing fresh plots of land, all the others said they would continue to do garden work. The estate plan was to extend their plots backwards or forwards as the case happened to be, according to how much was used up in the making of the road. So that really it turned out that they did not have to move any great distance and would be able to see the building operations while working on the land.

After compensation had been generously settled, they all thought the Americans would begin work at once. But days went by, and all that happened was another surveying party came and put down more pickets through the fields.

So they waited, and Tiger began slowly and painfully to write about how they had garden, but the Americans came and they had to move. He went to San Juan and into a store selling books and bought one about roads. He read next door in Joe's house in the night, and when Joe was ready to sleep and turned him out he raised the wick of the lamp in his own hut and sat down on the floor and read about roads, because he didn't want this thing to happen to him and not know anything about it.

CHAPTER EIGHT

The sun, almost halfway to the centre of the sky, seemed to lose intensity for a minute as a wind ran through the village, turned the leaves of the mangrove trees in the swamp and twisted the branches of the coconut palms, then spread out low and long as it reached the coast and the Gulf of Paria. The rigging in the schooners alongside the St. Vincent jetty in the harbour shook, a sail halfway up a mast flapped, and a barefooted Negro, a Grenadian, took a mouthful of water from an enamel cup and gargled, spouting the water over the side. He hawked and spat as far as he could and watched the wind ruffling the water.

A bus pulled out of the stand near the post office in San Juan, packed with workers for the city. "No mo' room, no mo' room," the conductor bawled as a man tried to hop on the bus. That part of San Juan near the main road was rammed with traffic and early vendors and people anxious to get to work on time. Taxis crawled, enticing passengers; some going into the farther country districts changed their minds and turned around in San Juan when they saw the amount of fares for the city. A driver, eating a roti for his breakfast, took up three and headed for the city. He stopped at sixth avenue in Barataria for another. Housewives were buying early, crowding around

Joseph's meat stall, and he stood surveying them indifferently, sharpening his knife. Lettuce and water cress were going cheap; a donkey cart laden with coconuts was doing good business; the driver, his roti eaten, asked the passengers to please wait a minute while he drank a coconut. A local train slowed down and stopped at the halt. The guard had forgotten to close the gates on the other side of the street, but a pedestrian did it for him just as the train groaned to a halt. Scores of young girls who worked in the stores in Frederick Street, students for the colleges, manual labourers, all got on, and the guard waved a ragged green flag and the train blew smoke in the wind and started off slowly, for there was another halt about three hundred yards down, in tenth avenue. The taxi driver finished his coconut and joined the stream of traffic. "Look, de Americans starting to build dey road," he told his passengers as he stopped for a young coloured girl. They saw machinery and a few Americans in blue dungarees. The girl sat in the front seat, sweeping her hands under her skirt so it wouldn't crumple as she sat. The train jogged through the swamp, behind a rum bond and a coconut-oil factory where they made tins. The taxi driver swerved from a bus and narrowly escaped an oncoming truck; the coloured girl held her breath. He reached the bus stop before the bus and took up a manual labourer in dirty clothes. The girl sniffed as he got in beside her and drew as near as she could to the driver. The train ran alongside a canal filled with nasty water at the edge of the swamp. The wind went in at one side, fanning the crowded compartments, and blew out the windows. The taxi stopped in Marine Square and the girl got out. It would have been nearer her place of work if she had got off in George Street, but she couldn't bear to walk there. She always got off in the square and walked down and turned right into the shopping centre. The train whistled and the station exuded passengers. Men and women hurried off to work and students caught tram-cars to go to school.

The Grenadian seaman, having washed his face, went to the stern of the schooner and loosened his trousers and stooped over the side, holding on to a stay.

Urmilla took a rest from sweeping the yard and watched Chandra crawling on the floor. She sat on the back steps, under the shade of the mango tree, and the child came to her and she lifted it in her arms. "You hungry, dou-dou?" She stroked the baby's head. Every night she anointed Chandra with coconut oil to keep her healthy. She pulled out a brown, full breast and put the teat to the baby's mouth. Chandra closed her eyes and sucked, her little fingers and toes twitching with pleasure. "That nough," Urmilla said and put the baby down and fixed herself. "I have to go and graze the cow now. But I won't stay too long. You must sleep in the hammock until I come back."

She was always lonely when Tiger was away, and she had taken to talking out loud as she worked. Once Rita heard her and stood up, listening. "And when we get money," she was telling the child, "we moving from here, and going in a pretty house to live. And plenty of nice things for you to wear. Little dresses and shoes—look up to now you ain't have a pair of shoes, don't mind you can't walk yet, but still!" "Aaye, gul, yuh mad or wat, talking to yuhself?" Rita had asked. Urmilla saw her and blushed. "I only talking to Chandra, man," she said.

She never liked to talk about herself or how she felt about the future. Not even Tiger knew what she thought about; he thought she was stupid. When in the night he told her how life would be different when they had money, she didn't tell him anything. Where was all this money to come from? He never told her. He just said, "Girl, one day things go be different, you just wait and see."

She put Chandra in the hammock, tying the loose ends

together, and gave it a shove. It swung, and the baby's eyes opened wide, puzzled by the movement.

Urmilla took the cow and walked slowly down the street, stopping to allow it to crop at green patches of grass near the drains. She saw a vacant house, and the gate was open. She went in and left the cow in the yard, walking around and looking at the glass windows and the painted walls. Such a house would be better to live in than a stupid old mud hut. It had electric light and water—Tiger wouldn't have to get up extra early to catch water at the standpipe. Every night now he sitting up late reading with the lamp, his eyes would go bad. What he reading? He say he learning to read. She sat on the back steps, rubbing a stick against the concrete. Why he learning to read? So he could be a big man and have education. So when they get this money, and living in big house, he wouldn't be stupid. But Rita say he is a damn fool. She say Joe can't read so good, or write, and how they have a good house, and Joe have a job with the base? But still, she well sending Henry to school to learn, though!

She saw bhagi—an edible plant—growing wild. She picked the good ones, looking in the road to see if anybody was watching. She went to the front and tiptoed in the gallery to peer in a window. The house was unfurnished. She saw the drawing and dining rooms. The doors to the bedrooms were locked. Once, while selling milk, she had seen the interior of a well-furnished house. The woman had told her to wait while she went inside for money, leaving the door open. And Urmilla had seen. Big upright chairs in which she could sleep, with soft, pretty cushions. Pictures on the wall. Vases with flowers. A piano shining in the corner. A table with Christmas cards. And the dining room behind. A mahogany table polished to clear reflection. A dumbwaiter with so many things! Glasses and jugs and pretty silver things to hold things, and a big looking-glass in the centre! She used after that to look in all the houses where she sold milk, drawing comparisons. Rita's house wasn't so nice, Joe was always dirtying it up. When we get house, that will be thing! A big piano, a big table—everything big, because is only when you small you does have small thing, and when you poor.

She stopped at Tall Boy's shop and asked him if he had got saltfish yet.

She thought of Tiger again as she pulled the cow along; it wanted to stop and eat everything, as if it was never satisfied. She had gone to the garden one day and seen Tiger arguing with an ochro tree. "Look, is time you start to bear," he was saying. "I give you good care, and I know you getting good food, because I do everything the government man say to do. Everybody ochro tree bearing, and you have to bear too, that is the reason why I plant you." She asked him if he wanted any help and he had shaken his head. "But what you could do," he said, "is go down by Deen and tell him to send my blasted hoe. He borrow it since day before yesterday, and I want it to use right now." She held her hands to her forehead and looked down the fields and said, "Like he wife using it now." Tiger said, "Don't mind that. So what? I must do without my own thing when I want it? Man, go and tell him to give it to you now now." Deen, pulling weeds with his hands, had said his wife was using it, if Tiger couldn't wait. "Yuh mean he can't wait little bit? Every day he does ask me for manure or seed. Wen Ah borrow anyting from him, he doing as if Ah tief it!" She had gone back and told Tiger. He listened. Too many damn people taking him for little boy still. Doing him as they like. His own hoe too besides! And Deen lie if he say I ever borrow thing from him. The most is some ochro seed he give me, and look, this tree like it don't want to bear, the damn seeds must be rotten! He had gone to Deen and pulled the hoe

from the woman's hands before she knew what he was doing.
"But, Tiger, dat is all de manners yuh have!" Deen's wife exclaimed. "Yuh so impatienate yuh can't wait little bit?" Deen
said, "Is all right, give de bitch he hoe. He go want someting
from we again." Tiger said, "Man, is two days straight you
have my hoe, you think is only you have place to weed?" Deen
was a much bigger man, with hairy arms and legs. Urmilla had
stood and looked on from a distance, afraid they were going to
fight. She went up to Tiger and said, "Come, let we go. Don't
bother with them." They walked away, and Deen's wife said,
"Look at she, she like a force-ripe mango!" Tiger spun around.
"She don't whore, though! I hear every night when Deen gone
San Juan or Port of Spain, you does have another man in the
house!" Urmilla tugged his arm. "Come and go," she said
urgently. Deen said, "Boy, yuh lucky yuh so small, Ah woudda
kill yuh here today!" The other gardeners had murmured to
themselves. Old Sookdeo hopped about. "Is long time Ah not
see fight dis side. Beat him up, Tiger! Beat him up, Deen!"
Sookdeo stumbled onto a lettuce bed and a man cursed him.
Sookdeo threatened to fight and they all laughed. Tiger walked
away, Urmilla clinging to his arm. When they got back to the
garden he said, "You yourself, you not have anything to do
home? You don't fraid something happen to the child?" She
had gone home to cook something nice for him, so he wouldn't
be vexed any more when his belly was full.

Suddenly she realized she wanted to talk to Rita. She
dragged the cow the rest of the way and peeped into the hut
to see if Chandra was asleep. Rita told her to come over, as she
was cooking calallo and couldn't leave the pot just now.

"Girl, I don't know how I forget to tell you bout what happen the other day in the garden! Deen did want to beat Tiger
for he own hoe!"

Rita stirred the pot and took out a spoonful of calallo. She wiped her hand on her dress and poured the sauce in her hand and licked it. She smacked her lips and turned to Urmilla.

"Now, let me hear dis scandal! Is wat happen, gul?"

Urmilla recounted the incident, and Rita said, "Tiger shudda bus' de hoe in 'e head. Das why it never good to lend ting out. Is all right like we so, but some people like dey don't have conscience. Yuh hear wat happen to Joe down at de base?"

"No, man."

"Well, yuh know he have ah good work wid de Yankees? People from all about going for work in de base, because de Yankee paying plenty money. American people not cheap like British people, gul! From de time people hear bout Yankee work, dey leaving everyting else, post office and treasury and government work, because dey getting more money dan de government cud pay. So wat yuh tink happen? De government say, 'Eh-heh! Is so?' And now dey pass ah new rule, telling de Americans dey can't pay so much money to de poor people, dat it upsetting 'conomy and society! And besides dat, at first de Americans used to pay in American money—yuh never see American money?"

Urmilla shook her head, and Rita took the pot off the fire and they went inside and sat in the drawing room. She opened her purse and showed Urmilla an American dollar.

"Yuh see dat dere?—well it worth bout one and ah half of we government dollar. So wen yuh get about twenty ah dem, it just as if yuh have forty! Well, on top of wat Ah tell yuh just now, de government say dat Trinidadians—and all dem small-island people—must not get pay in Yankee money. So yuh cud imagine how Joe vex like hell. Everybody vex."

"But how they could do the people that?"

"Ah don't know, but it done. Ah sorry for all dem Grenadians and St. Lucians who come over here to make money. If yuh see at small-island people in town! All over de place, way-ever yuh turn, yuh bouncing up small-island. Dey must be tink Trinidad is ah paradise."

"So what happen? Joe looking for new work?"

"Nar, man. He still working down in de base, but it have ah rumour spreading dat dey going to lay off men, and 'e might lose de job. Listen, yuh have any tomatoes to sell?"

"Yes, plenty. Corn too."

"Go bring ah pound for me, nar. Here, look ah shilling."

"No man, Rita, I won't charge you for it, man. You does give me so much thing whenever you have. If things was really bad I would take it."

"It ain't ah matter of dat. Allyuh have to make ah living by selling tings, and wen it come to business, it ain't have no friend-ship in dat. So take de shilling, gul. Ah know if yuh cudda afford it yuh wud give me everyting for nutting."

But Urmilla went away without taking the money and brought back a paper bag filled with the best tomatoes she had. "Here, one day when things really hard up I will come for the shilling."

Rita put the tomatoes in the kitchen. "So Tiger learning to read?"

"Yes, ain't he does come over here in the night to see?"

Rita laughed. "Imagine ah big man like he learning to read. How bout you, yuh don't want to learn too?"

"Who me? No, man." Urmilla looked round the room as if she had forgotten something. Then she exclaimed, "But you know, I forget the most important thing! Girl, I didn't have those things last week."

"Wat yuh mean? Oh-ho! It was yuh period?"

"Yes, is around that time."

"Up to now, nutting happen?"

"No."

"Well, must be another little Tiger on de way! But yuh can't be too sure. Some people does skip, yuh know. Wait until next month, nar. But is time yuh had ah next baby, anyway! Sometimes Ah wish Ah was able, but it look like Ah wud never have any. Joe say he don't mind, he say he glad, dat children is trouble. But Ah ain't minding he, nar. One ah dese days Ah go take up meself and go to see ah doctor and find out if anyting wrong wid me."

"Girl, Tiger so funny these days. I don't know how to tell him. I don't know if he go be glad or vex."

"Well, yuh not sure yet, so yuh don't have to tell him right now. Wait little bit until yuh sure, nar, den yuh cud tell him. If is anyting Ah hope is ah boy dis time. De last time he nearly dead wen 'e hear was ah gul! Yuh remember de night?"

"You think I will ever forget? You was really good to me, Rita. You is a true friend."

"Ah, don't talk stupidness. People must live good wid dey neighbour. Ah like yuh and Tiger, Ah don't know why. Allyuh does live good."

"But since he learning things he like he forgetting me and the baby."

"Well, is so life is sometimes. He now growing up like ah man, yuh know. Wen he pass dat stage he go be like de old Tiger yuh used to know."

"So you advise me not to tell him anything now?"

"Look, gul, don't say dat! Yuh cud do wat yuh want to do, *oui!* Ah just tell yuh how I feel. Is up to yuh. If yuh want to tell him, is your business. But Ah don't like to advise nobody bout nutting, because if anyting go wrong is I who go get blame. Don't mix me up in allyuh business, nar!"

Tiger said to the American officer, not waiting for Boysie to speak, "Just tell me what to do, and I will do it. I was reading a book on how to build road, so I know about it. Is true doing it is a different thing, but—"

The American, in charge of civilian labour, laughed. "Look, John—"

"I name Tiger."

"Well, whatever your name is. You just assist us, see? The foreman will tell you what to do. Obey orders, do what you're told, and we'll all get on fine. That goes for all of you." He eyed the civilians. "I don't want any trouble."

"Twenty dollar ah week!" Boysie told Tiger. "Dat is plenty money, yes. Dat is ah hundred dollar ah month. Is better pay dan Ah feel we wudda get."

"Imagine," Tiger told Urmilla after his first day's work, "how much thing we could do with that money. No wonder people leaving all other work to get American job! Today they had people from all in San Juan and Laventille, come to look for work. About twenty of we working now. The boss say later on when the work come more, they will take on more men. I hear tomorrow about forty more coming."

"Is what sort of work you doing?"

"All kinds of thing, man. Clearing away the bush, cutting down the bush with cutlass. You ever see what they call a bull-dozer?"

"What?"

"A bulldozer, man. If you see that thing work! The driver—is a creole man from St. Joseph, he know how to drive it—he does only have to drive straight up to a tree, and the bull-dozer push the tree, and it fall down! And it doing thing like digging dirt, and shovelling up, hmm, is a big invention, if they go on so they go make things to do all the work, and we wouldn't have no job!"

"I wish I could work too."

"Don't fraid, I know what you go do. We have some money

save from the compensation. You must make things to sell, the Americans would buy. You see how it have a Indian woman out by the main road, near sixth avenue, how she does make money for so, selling roti and thing? Well, you could do that too, down by where the road building. Plenty of the fellars who not living near does go in the parlour and eat bread and butter and drink sweet drink. If you could be near the job, you know how much money we make! Them Americans well like they curry and roti; I hear they does buy in Port of Spain and eat all about."

"I was thinking as we have this money we could repair the house little bit. We could buy galvanize sheet and put on the roof, and move all them old carat leaf. Because, Tiger, it go be such a long time before we have money enough to buy a house with."

"This old mud hut really bad. But I not spending any money on it. What you think I going to do with the first pay I get? Guess what?"

"I don't know."

"I starting to buy bricks! One by one I will buy. You know, I had a idea last night. Why we must buy a house? Why we can't build one, right here where the hut is? All we have to do is to make sure we could get the land, we could lease it from the estate. And I could build it myself, man! The men in the village go help me. Every payday I go buy something. Cement. More brick. Wood. Galvanize."

"Don't forget clothes for the children."

"Which children?"

"But how you playing as if you don't know I going to have another baby!"

"What the hell is this!" Tiger pushed back the chair he was sitting in and it toppled to the floor. "Is who tell you so? I bet is Rita!"

"Well, I did know for myself, but still I ask she, and she say yes, it on the way now, but is plenty time yet."

"When you find this thing out?"

"Few days now."

"You going mad or what? And all this time you didn't tell me nothing? Is only tonight you telling me?"

"But, Tiger, these days you so funny. You hardly home. You always busy, reading or writing, and you say I must keep quiet when you working. These days you so 'cited, you going all about in the night. You going to play cards with Boysie. You going in the shop. You going out with Joe. You going San Juan. You not paying attention to home. Last Sunday I don't know where you been, but you come home late, smelling of rum. Whole week you only talking about the road the Americans going to build. And I thought you did know for yourself, because you remember how Chandra come when we do the thing, and we does do it still, so child must come."

"Why you didn't tell me before?"

"I was fraid man, Tiger. You ain't vex with me for that? It don't make no difference, is a long time to go yet."

"Well, even the neighbours know my wife going to have child and I don't know! You looking for licks, yes? I mad to bust your mouth, I mad to kill you here with licks tonight!"

Urmilla cowered near the baby in the hammock. "But, Tiger—"

"I don't want to hear a damn thing, man! You feel as if you is a big woman, eh? You feel as if you could do thing without telling me? I bet I send you back to Chaguanas! I bet I do something to stop the baby from coming! It have ways, you know."

"Oh God, you mustn't say that, Tiger. If we father and mother hear you saying that—"

"To hell with them! They don't have nothing to do with

it! You think is all my life I go let them tell me what to do? From the time I small, they doing everything for me. They married me to you, and I didn't even know you, or where you come from. Up to now I don't know what sort of woman you really is! All now so, I could have been man, and I would have meet a girl I love, and get married to she when I could have afford it. You think they give me anything? They give me a cow and this old mud hut in Barataria, and they give me you. Look at you. You ain't have no sense, you ain't even pretty. Deen have a pretty wife. Boysie have a pretty girl in Port of Spain, don't mind she creole, he show me she photo. But I ask you again, is why you didn't tell me this thing before?"

"Oh God," Urmilla sobbed, "I beg you pardon."

"Don't think you go soften me up with them tears! You sure is my child you making? I not as stupid as before, you know. You sure is my child? You does be here home alone when I go out, you sure you didn't have anything to do with nobody?"

Urmilla hung her head in shame and sobbed, unable to speak.

Tiger went next door. "Rita, you did know Urmilla was going to have a baby?"

Rita was home alone. Joe had gone out and Henry was sleeping.

"Yes, wat happen?" she asked, seeing his agitation.

"And all this time you didn't tell me nothing? Is so you call yourself a friend?"

"Wat happen to yuh at all? Is why yuh so excited? Urmilla didn't tell yuh?"

"She now tell me."

"Well, wat happen for dat? Yuh was so busy wid yuh compensation business, and getting work wid de Americans, and reading yuh book, and writing yuh story—"

"What story?"

"How yuh mean? Ain't yuh writing ah story bout how all-yuh had to leave de garden, and how de road building?"

"Who tell you so—Urmilla?"

"And who else den? But wat happen to yuh, Tiger? Why yuh so hot tonight? Is wat do yuh?"

"Man, Rita, you didn't treat me like a friend at all. You mean since the other day you and she know about this baby, and nobody tell me anything at all? So what, so I ain't man in my own house now?"

"Yuh too damn foolish, yuh cud see yuh is ah little boy still. Dat ain't nutting to get so vex bout. She wudda tell yuh, but yuh playing big scholar, reading and writing, and dese days and nights yuh never home till late in de night."

"Like you know all my business."

"Ah know, oui! Everybody does know everybody else business in dis village. Yuh ain't nobody special nar, yuh just like one ah we. And too besides, look here, if you and yuh wife have quarrel, don't come over here and make no noise, yuh hear? Don't mind Joe ain't here, Ah will trow yuh out if yuh make too much noise!"

"All right, Rita, all right. I ain't quarrelling with you. It ain't your fault. But tell me"—and he lowered his voice, ripe with knowledge—"you never see anybody round here when I not home? You never notice if any man does come to see Urmilla when I out in the night or working in the day?"

"Wat yuh trying to say at all?"

"Girl, I not stupid as long time. Long time people could have fool me, because I didn't know things. But I know a lot now, how men does go round by other people wife when they husband not home, and have thing to do with them. You thought I didn't know! I could see you look surprise!"

"Yuh mean yuh tink Urmilla horning yuh, dat she have anoder man?" Rita asked incredulously.

"Well, it could happen you know. Plenty things could happen and nobody find out. Tell me girl, Rita, you never see anybody? Especially these nights?"

"Get out me blasted chair!" Rita shouted. "Get out de house, yuh worthless bitch! Yuh have a nasty coolie mind! Dat poor gul does only be tinking bout you all de time, how Tiger going to do dis for she, and dat for she. How Tiger working hard to save money to build house. And look at yuh, yuh nasty dog! Yuh suspect she horning yuh! Yuh ain't have no shame? Dat poor gul don't even look at any oder man but you, though she well have cause! And yuh know wat have yuh so? Yuh know why yuh mind turning nasty? Becasue yuh reading all dem book, because yuh finding out too much tings bout life. Dat's why. Learning to read! Learning to write! Why de hell yuh don't learn how to mind yuh wife? Ah wish it was true dat she horning yuh! Ah wish she had anoder man! Den yuh go stop reading dem book and going all bout in de night for experience! Yuh is a damn fool. Ah had ah mind once yuh wud turn out to be ah good husband, but wat yuh say here tonight really shame me. Get out de house, man. Haul yuh tail from here, don't stay here, go someway else."

CHAPTER NINE

The nearest Trinidad ever got to actual warfare was one dark night in 1942. An enemy submarine sneaked into the harbour and blasted two ships at anchor. The explosions shook the city. No one knew what it was about, but terror remained for a few days. A compulsory service bill was never proclaimed because there were sufficient volunteers. Later that year the western coast of the island was mined, and entrances to the harbour closed to shipping, and night sailings by coastal steamers stopped. By this time 15,000 people formerly engaged in food production had either joined the forces or were working with the Yanks. Foodstuffs were subsidized by the government to keep down prices. In a queue for bread at a baker's in George Street a fight broke out between two men and one ran for the cutlass which a coconut vendor had stuck in his donkey cart. At least three marriages were hastened because the girls were pregnant. Tentative programmes of essential works were drawn up in anticipation of unemployment when work on the bases ceased. American authorities agreed to a methodical release of labour so as not to disturb the economic system. The sugar crop dropped to a low level because no one wanted to work in the fields again, but shipping difficulties prevented the export of the reduced quantity and the population was urged to consume more sugar. Steps were being taken to introduce rationing. A tiny island called Patos, midway between the capital and the mainland of Venezuela, was handed over to the Venezuelan Foreign Minister. Hooliganism increased.

Tiger refused to think about the baby. Somehow he felt he had done wrong by speaking to his wife and neighbour the way he did, accusing Urmilla of being unfaithful. But he righted the wrong in his mind, arguing that all sorts of things had to happen, not just good all the time. And he hadn't struck Urmilla, he had just threatened her—all of that was good for a man to do his wife sometimes. Look at Rita, with all she talk look how much time she and Joe don't fight, Joe does cuff she up and kick she up and leave she bawling on the ground. Joe don't be home, nearly every night he in town having a good time with he friends. What she playing at all? Man, one time I see Deen give he wife one kick, in front of everybody, because she come in the shop when he drinking and ask him for money. Look how much thing other people does do. And what I do? I only ask she if she sure is my baby. Boysie did telling me how one time a girl try to stick him with a child, and it wasn't he own. He tell me I must watch out for that kind of thing. Man, people too worthless, yes! You have to be on guard all the time.

It was towards the end of the rainy season. For some reason which Tiger did not know the road had to be built in a great hurry. Well, he would work in a hurry. He discovered that if he worked hard it kept his mind off thinking.

They started off by clearing the bush. None of the villagers had ever seen a bulldozer before, and to see it in action was to them an amazing thing. There were two of them, one driven by an American. Tiger thought he would like to learn to

drive, if they would let him. He felt power in the machinery.
With a root-puller attached, the tractor would move up to a
tree and the arms would reach down into the earth and wrest
the tree out.

"Yuh see how Yankee does work, boy," Boysie told Tiger.
"Only modern tings here. It wudda take two three men half-
day to cut dat tree down and dig out de root; it only take de
Yankee machine five minute."

All day the noise and clatter of machinery at work was
heard. Working gangs were organized. Tiger found himself
with nine others, some of whom he knew by sight, the others
were natives out of the village. But that first week he didn't
work very hard because he was thinking too much about what
was happening, and watching on at operations. By the end
of the week they had cleared roughly a thirty-yard-wide strip
from the main road, and were working on his plot of land as
if a garden had never been there. A tractor levelled down the
beds on which he had planted lettuce at one time; he saw earth
where melongene and tomatoes grew change shape, scooped
up into the air and flung to one side. And he thought how
after one time, is another. In one week the landscape was
showing the colour of the naked brown earth and the deep
impressions of the tractors. Landmarks familiar to him—a coconut tree near the edge of the swamp, a ricefield—were buried
under the powerful machinery as they advanced.

"You mean," Tiger asked a fellow worker, "that that bulldozer could root anything from out of the ground?"

"Well, no. I uses to work down in de base, and it have
some root dat so deep in de ground dat we had was to blow
dem up wid dynamite. Dat was big-time work, boy. Up here
ain't nothing, man. Dem scraggy tree, looking desperate, is
nutting for de bulldozer to lick down."

One morning as a native foreman was sending off a working party an American corporal came up and put his hands on his hips and looked them over.

"You there—the young Indian—what did you say your name is?"

"Is Tiger, chief."

"Tiger what?"

"Just Tiger, chief. Everybody call me so."

"Okay. Want to work with the surveying party?"

"Yes, chief, if you think I could do the work."

"Come on then, all you have to do is carry a tripod."

"Like yuh getting promotion, boy," someone said, and the whole gang laughed.

It was advance work for him now, working ahead of the gangs. He carried a tripod. He was the only native working with the surveying party. One of the two American surveyors explained, "This is the tripod. You'll carry that, and don't lag, keep up with us all the time. This is a staff, these are pegs. And this"—holding it carefully under his arm—"is a theodolite. Gotta be careful with this, bud. You don't meddle with it at all unless we tell you to, see?"

Tiger nodded, though he would have liked more explanation.

The party stood at a distance and surveyed Sookdeo's garden. The land was proving to be soft and muddy here because a ricefield was adjacent. The surveyors talked among themselves, and Tiger stood a respectable distance off, but he could hear them plainly. And suddenly he had a fear that something was going to happen to Sookdeo's land. He had to find out.

"Chief, the road going to build on that garden too?"

"Looks like it, John," the American replied.

"But, chief, first time when they measure the land they say

Sookdeo garden could stay! All of we had to move but they say Sookdeo could stay, that the road won't pass through he land."

"Well, I'll tell you what, John. Know what we'd do? We'd make a big curve, and cut into the swamp, and we wouldn't bother Sookdeo. How's that?"

"Chief, give me a minute off, please? Just let me run in the village and tell him? He is my friend, he is a old man. It won't take me long, chief, I sure to meet him by the shop or by sixth avenue, selling."

The Americans looked at the concern on Tiger's face, and one of them said, "Okay, but hurry up, they're going to move in on that land now!"

Tiger rested the tripod gently on the ground and took off at top speed, running through the bush.

He was gasping when he reached Sookdeo's hut.

"Where you father, girl, answer quick!" he said to Dolly, kneading flour in the kitchen.

"Ah don't know. He must be out by de main road or in de shop. Yuh didn't pass by Tall Boy? But wat it is happen?"

He ran on the grass at the side of the road to save cutting his feet on the stones. He didn't know if to try the shop or the main road, they were both equidistant. He was almost to the main road when he changed his mind and cut across seventh street and made for the shop.

Sookdeo was sitting on a soapbox, reading the papers.

Tiger was out of breath and couldn't say a word. He just stood there panting, and Sookdeo said, "Wat happen, boy? Yuh in ah fight? Wat yuh running so for?"

"The garden," Tiger gasped. "It going. You have to move."

"Yuh talkam nonsense!" the old man exclaimed, "me gettam no notice."

"I tell you it going, Sookdeo! The surveyors must be tell the working gang to move up already! I was with them! They say bout half the garden have to go!"

Sookdeo sat as if glued to the box. An ashen pallor crept into his face. He blinked his eyes. His hands began to shake.

"Not true," he muttered, "not true." But his whole body showed belief. He was shaking. He got off the box and held on to Tiger.

"Dey start already, yuh say? Dey moveam big tractor and engine my garden side?"

"Yes, Sookdeo. Come and go now, man, and get what you could. They not going to hold up the work for tomatoes and lettuce. But you sure to get plenty compensation, as all of we get. But come quick. I will help you reap whatever bearing."

Sookdeo came to life. "Oh gawd oh!" he cried and ran out of the shop.

Tiger slowed down to keep with him. "What happen so suddenly?" he asked.

"Boy, me just remember—" He tried to run faster. "Come quick, Tiger, yuh running too slow, man!"

A bulldozer moved. Sookdeo saw it, getting nearer and nearer. And he couldn't run any more. He walked in quick jerky steps, talking to himself. "De money. Oh gawd oh, de money dat Ah bury. Dey go get it! Dem tief! Dey go tief me money. Oh gawd oh!"

Before he reached the clearing he began to shout. "Hold up! Hold up! Wait right dere! Hold up dat 'dozer business! Give me ah chance, boss. Wait for me!"

The mango tree was in fruit. The workers looked at the ripe yellow mangoes dangling on long stems. They pelted stones and caught the fruit as they fell.

The old man's shouts were drowned in the noise of the tractor as the American manoeuvred the machine expertly and brought it to within a foot of the tree.

Sookdeo, his breath coming in gasps and sobs, scrambled over his beds, trampling young plants. He slipped on a heap of wet cow dung and cursed loudly in Hindi as he fell and rolled. He didn't get up. He continued to roll until he was at the foot of the mango tree, to the amazement and amusement of the working party.

"Hey, Ram," the American shouted from the tractor, "save yourself there! Want me to make a hamburger outa you?"

But Sookdeo began digging in the earth with his bare hands. He was frantic. He didn't say a word. He just looked up now and again as his hands scooped the dry earth like a garden fork, to make sure the 'dozer business wasn't advancing.

The driver was looking at him and scratching his head. "What gives?" he asked. "You got something buried there, bud?"

Sookdeo glared and went on digging, his hands working like pistons, his nails broken.

Tiger borrowed a cutlass from one of the men and said, "Let me help you dig, Sookdeo. Is what you have bury there?"

But Sookdeo only snatched the cutlass from his hand and stabbed it in the earth, and the labourers gathered around him, joking about how Indian people like to bury their money, they were sure he had some buried under the tree.

Dry sounds came from his throat. He hurled the cutlass behind him and reached into the hole and drew out the Oval-tine tin. He was past caring now. He prised open the lid, and everyone crowded round to see, and the American said, "Holy smoke!"

Sookdeo counted the money with bleeding fingers. And

when he was sure none had been stolen, he raised his head and shouted.

"All right! Bring machine now! Move tree! Break up garden! Nobody tief Sookdeo money, though! American tief want to take Sookdeo money, eh? Bring 'dozer to root up mango tree, eh? Money safe, though! Build road all about now, Sookdeo don't care! Sookdeo have money!"

And with tears streaming down his face like a baby the old man stumbled away from the labourers, and some of them laughed and the others were silent, and the American driver shook his head and murmured, "Gee!"

Tiger put his arms around the old man's shoulders. "Is all right, Sookdeo, nobody want to thief you money, nobody did know it was there."

But Sookdeo only cried, all the strength gone from his body. He put the bills in his pocket and threw away the tin.

"Come, man, let we go and fire a drink at Tall Boy," Tiger suggested in an effort to revive his spirits.

But for the first time in his life Sookdeo refused to have a drink of rum.

"No, boy, no," he sobbed. "Everything gone and done for dis old man now. Time for Sookdeo to dead. Garden gone, nutting to do. Long time now everybody saying, 'But look at Sookdeo! Yuh mean he still alive?' Well, soon Sookdeo dead. No more old man for de children to make joke at. No more Sookdeo drunk in de canal and people have to carry him home. Sookdeo dead, dead, dead."

It was as if he were weeping at his own funeral.

"Well, all right then, let me carry you home. You go and sleep, tomorrow you go feel better. Don't fraid, you will get good compensation money. All of us get plenty, and your garden was bigger than mine. You could make a start on a fresh piece of land. Man, you won't even have to move, the estate people will just extend you garden backward some more, and you could see how we building the road even while you working in you garden! You still strong man, don't mind what people say! Who in Barataria could drink more rum than Sookdeo? Who does have the best crop, the best tomatoes, tomatoes so big that one, two, three weighing a pound! You remember what you tell me the other night? Man, you could plant things and they would come anywhere! It might be you even get a better land, where the soil richer. Just now the rainy season go finish and you could prepare the land for planting. Man, you still strong, yes! I had trouble keeping up with you when we was running just now! I wish I was as strong as you! You go and sleep, don't worry bout anything. Tomorrow you go feel better."

But tomorrow Sookdeo didn't feel better. He dreamed in the night that a big 'dozer came up behind him while he was working in the ricefield, and when he turned round, the 'dozer scooped him up and flung him far into the swamp, over the coconut trees and the mangroves. Then, after that, he dreamed how he was in the canefields when his parents had brought him from India to work in Trinidad. He was in the canefields, and an American came and said, "Hey, you're Sookdeo?" And when he said yes, the American said, "All right, we want you!" And he kept on saying we want you we want you we want you, and he ran into a patch of canes to hide. But they came after him, in 'dozers. The 'dozers trampled the canes, the sticky juice ran into the soil. And he was trying to do something before they came for him. He was burying money. If even they got him, they wouldn't get the money. He could hear the noise coming, the canes groaning as they toppled down before the giants. . . . He was in Tall Boy's shop, reading the papers. "What news about China, Sookdeo?" the China-man asked, and he read, full of pride because he could read.

Don't mind Sookdeo always drunk, he could read though, it
have plenty people who does laugh at him, but they can't
read! Read the news, Sookdeo. Show them that you not a fool
as they think. What happening with the war? Who winning?
the British or the German? . . . The sun spun crazily in the
sky, like it had gone mad. It burned him. It had been burning
him ever since he could remember. But he loved it, because
everything looked good when it was shining. And the wind
came all the way from the swaying canefields in the south of
the island where he had burned away his youth, to the village,
spreading out and sending brown leaves whirling in the air.
Round and round and round. . . . He was drinking rum now.
By the gallons. But he couldn't feel as he used to feel, no matter
how much he drank. He could see Tall Boy pouring it out
for him, it poured amber. Pour a full drink, man, give me a
double shot. Who in Barataria could drink more rum than
Sookdeo? Everybody have drinks on me. Look how much
compensation money I get, more than all of you put together!
Come, Deen, come, Rajnauth, come, Tiger, come, Boysie,
even creole come! Come, Joe, fire one with the old man! Don't
mind you is creole and I is coolie! Everybody must live good
together as friend! The rum poured from huge barrels, but
he couldn't get enough. Is what happen to this rum at all, Tall
Boy? Like you mixing it with water! Bring the strongest rum
you have, man. He lifted the counter and went into the shop
and opened the top of a barrel. Dark, mellow, cool, the rum
looked to him. He had never seen so much rum at one time.
He put his head down in it and drank. Everybody laughed
to see. He drank, drank, drank. . . . He was at Seta's wedding.
And all the time he thought he was drunk! "Look *bap* come!"
he heard Dolly whisper to his wife. "Look how he dress up!"
No old clothes that he beg people for. No old khaki pants and
tear-up merino, dirtying up with mud. He have on clean *dhoti,*

and turban, and sandal. Everybody surprised to see how Sookdeo dress up so. Which part he get money from? They asking
one another. But he not paying them any mind at all. The
wedding taking place in Barataria. He have a big tent put up
behind the hut, decorate with flowers and bamboo and coconut branch. Is the biggest wedding they ever see, and is
Sookdeo who in charge of everything. People so surprise they
can't even talk! Big shots from all about come to Sookdeo
daughter wedding. And now, is time for the feast. Everybody
must eat. Food so much that they must have to eat they belly
full and it still have plenty. The whole village lining up for
food at Sookdeo daughter wedding. Sookdeo stand up and
look to see everything going right. He see so much creole mix
up with the Indian people! Because creole and Indian does live
good, and creole does go to all them Indian ceremonies. But it
look as if they rushing for the food, man. So is Sookdeo who
have to put them in order. Sookdeo raise he hand and everybody look at him. "What matter rush?" Sookdeo asked the people. "Who time Indian people have them thing, seeam creole
from all about come. But who time creole have them thing, no
seeam any Indian! Creole, fall back. Fall back, and let them
Hindian come beforehand!" They must listen to Sookdeo, yes.
Everything in order now, and everybody eating they belly
full. Then afterwards, Mr. Bunsee get up to make a speech.
Mr. Bunsee say he proud to be at Sookdeo daughter wedding,
and how he have a surprise for Mr. Sookdeo. He say that he
have the compensation money to give Sookdeo. And Sookdeo
going for this money quick. He have on old clothes again, and
he barefoot like he does always be, but he ain't minding them
at all. Is the money he want. He stretching out he hand, but
Mr. Bunsee making joke. Every time he go to reach it, Mr.
Bunsee pulling he hand away. Give me my money, man. Is my
own. Americans come and take the land, is my money. You

hear? Stop playing the fool, man. Is my money, is mine, is mine, is mine . . .

Cutting up the trunk of the mango tree the next day, a labourer's axe bit into the bark and split the mark Sookdeo had made when he buried the money. Trucks took the debris away.

News of Sookdeo's death depressed Tiger and for some days he did no reading or writing. There had been something about the old man, a hidden pride, a secret knowledge. And Tiger had never known him to worry until these last weeks. He felt he understood Sookdeo more than anybody else, that he had sympathized while others scorned and laughed, that he had been, in a way, a companion, someone to talk to, to share secrets with (don't mind he didn't tell me about the money he bury under the mango tree), a friend with whom to drink. And, above all that, it was Sookdeo who had inspired and helped him to read.

He went to the hut and saw the old man, stiff, his eyes and mouth open. His wife and daughter wept copiously. In life he was to be scorned and argued with every minute of the day. In death he was to be mourned, the good he did remembered. A stream of villagers flowed gently into the hut with sympathetic remarks. Poor Sookdeo dead. He was ah good man. Don't mind he drink plenty rum, he still ah good man. They stood about, flowing into the corners, and they murmured to Sookdeo's wife that if she wanted any help they were there to give it. But she said the government people would bury him, that they wouldn't have no trouble. Oh gawd oh, but wat ah go do, Sookdeo gone. Wat ah go do! Is only me and Dolly here now!

Tiger thought about death; he was young and strong and could afford to shrug at it. But how about when he got old as Sookdeo, gnarled and bent, wizened and sunburned. What about Urmilla and the children when he died? Sookdeo had buried some money, and the compensation would keep his family for a while; there were always jobs to do in the village, they would get by. But supposing he died and didn't leave any money at all for Urmilla. He would have to plan for the future. What was he going to do with all the money he would make working for the Americans? He would go away and study. No. He would stay and build house. Nar, man. Buy plenty land, have big garden. Nar. Send the children to Port of Spain to get big education, come doctor and lawyer. Open up a shop and make more money. Send Urmilla and the children back to Chaguanas and go away to another land with Boysie. See America. Go England.

It was the sun brought him out of depression, shining warmly in the sky. It was the sun cast the labourers' shadows on the ground, so they worked on their heads and shoulders, and curved their arms over their faces and wiped away perspiration; the Americans used handkerchiefs. And he reconciled himself to Sookdeo's death by reasoning thus: God, is why you kill Sookdeo? Because he is a old man, and everything have to dead when it get old. When the bodee vine finish bearing, it does dead. Everything does dead when it finish doing what it have to do. Sookdeo work, he get married, he have children. He keep garden. He live till he get old, then he dead. But he do what he come on earth for? Is how I go know that? Everybody come to work—look even white American working, and in Port of Spain, them rich people does have things to do too. And what again? Well, different things. Some people does married and have children, some does go away and study lawyer and doctor, some does go and live in other country. Is what I going to do? Is what I must do before I dead? Man, I don't know. I can't bother my head with all of that one time. I go have to wait and see what happen. Sometimes things does happen to you and you don't have anything to do with it, like how I get married and come up here to live.

He took up the tripod and followed the surveyors. The job of going ahead and feeling out the land gave him a feeling of importance. He knew he was doing something much bigger than just manual labour.

"How you don't know," he told Urmilla, "I so good at the job now that chief say I could carry the theodolite! That is something they have to be careful with, you know—long time only the Americans used to carry it. But chief call me today. He say, 'John'—I don't know why he like to call me so—He say, 'John, you could start carrying the theo. You're very ambitious, John,' he say. He say he keep an eye on me. I might get promotion, girl."

Sometimes he rode in a jeep, sometimes in a Mack truck. But always he was in advance of the other workers, and he felt as if he were one of the surveyors too, laying down the road, making plans for others to work on. One mile down, into the grove of bamboos growing so tall they groaned and squeaked in the wind. Over the San Juan river, where it curved near the back of the village. Every day now he was far from home, but the jeep took him back quickly. He was getting to know the workmen, he was familiarizing himself with how the work was progressing, sort of reasoning out things for himself, thinking, The road can't pass here because the land too soft— it would sink in the rainy season. And he told chief too, and he told them about the trees, and the village, and when he was a little boy, and about Sookdeo, how he buried money under the mango tree in his garden. He was getting so he wasn't afraid to talk now. People can't do you anything when you talk. And if you tell them things they will tell you things too, and so you could learn. Chief is a good man, don't mind he white. And Larry, the other American, he all right too. He does give me Lucky Strike cigarettes and chewing gum and ask the most questions.

The natives working on the road called one another Joe and imitated the Yankee drawl. Get a move on there, bud. We gotta work in a hurry. And they bought Yankee sailor caps and army caps off the servicemen, and wore them proudly in the village and at work.

So colourful September came with its short Indian summer. Tiger saw the farmers busy in their gardens; every day he would watch them and wish bountiful crops. Now that he was not toiling on the land himself he appreciated the difficulties of it. He found it hard to believe that he had depended on his crops for a livelihood. It was too much hard work. He wouldn't go back to gardening again. When he had his house and a piece of land, he would just grow fruit trees because he loved to see things come up out of the earth, not to sell. A little rain fell during those weeks. Not enough to cause any disruption of working operations, but to swell seeds sufficiently so they came up to see the sun. The earth was dug up on either side and thrown in the centre, and the road took rough shape, slightly higher than the land level. As the bulldozers emptied the earth, tractors ran up and down to compress the surface.

Tiger wrote down everything in his copybook. When he read over what he had written he realized that he didn't know any big words at all, except the names of the equipment they were working with. This was a bad thing. All the books he read had big words, and he had to use a dictionary to see what they meant. He could understand some and could spell them, but he couldn't use them. He would have to practise while talking to people. He memorized a few words from the dictionary every night. But while he was learning words he ignored grammar.

"Urmilla," he said, "you know what this thing I telling you about is for? I mean the theodolite."

"Ain't you say is that they does use to survey the land?"

"Yes, but I was wrong." He swallowed and tried to remember.

"Is a surveying instrument for measuring horizontal and vertical angles by means of telescope."

"Oh—ho, so is that! So they don't measure the land with it then?"

"No. So you see is a important thing that I does have to carry! Now, I will try you out with a little word. What it is 'to buy'?"

"Oh, that easy, man. That is when you go in the shop and buy anything, and you pay for it. That mean you buy it."

"Well, you have the idea, but you still not correct! To buy is to obtain by paying a price!"

"But ain't is the same thing I say, Tiger?"

"How is the same thing? You must learn to express yourself good, girl, like me. I will catch you with a easy one now! Every day people passing selling fish—look we just eat some for dinner. You know what a fish is?"

"But how? Is a thing that does live in the sea, and in river and pond too. It does swim, and people does eat it for food. Some of them have scale on them."

"I know I would catch you! You really wrong this time! The dictionary ain't say anything like that! It say is a animal living in water, is a vertebrate, cold-blooded animal having gills throughout life and limbs, if any, modified into fins. You see!"

"But man, Tiger, why you want to find out all of that for? I don't know what all them big word mean, man. It getting me puzzle up."

"Is the same thing I tell you. If you don't have education, people could always tie you up. All the time I did think a fish was just like what you say, but now I find out for truth what it really is! Look, hand me my small cylinders of narcotic rolled in paper."

"Cylinder? What is that? Is what you mean at all?"

Tiger chuckled, self-contented. "Just extend the terminal part of your arm, the extent of space between where you is and which part it is is not remote."

"I beg you pardon, Tiger, but I really don't know what you mean. This time you really tie me up!"

Tiger chuckled again. "All right, girl. Reach the cigarettes for me, then."

"Well," Urmilla said, "if you did say so all the time, now so you smoking already! Man," she said, handing him the pack, "I don't like this business. Too much thing coming between we. If you go on so, I won't understand anything you say."

"You better understand!" Tiger said meaningfully. "This morning I ask chief and Mr. Larry if they would like to eat Indian food, and he say sure, John. So tomorrow I bringing the two Americans home after work."

Urmilla gasped. "But what is this—"

"Shut up," Tiger said. "You have to cook like you never cook in you life before. The best things. Grind the massala yourself, don't buy curry powder from Tall Boy. Get *achar*, get *dhal*, and make *dhal pourri*. Make *meetai*. Fry *channa*. Buy two fowl from Deen wife. Buy a new wick for the lamp. Look, you don't want me to tell you what to do! And, girl, you better don't let anything go wrong, you hear. Them people is my boss, and if I please them good, I might get promotion."

"Oh God, but Tiger—"

"I don't want to hear nothing at all at all! Spend money, don't fraid. Go San Juan early and buy a new sari to put on, you must look good. And don't stop barefooted. Buy shoes. Buy a dress for the baby."

Urmilla hardly slept for thinking of what she was going to do. She got up determined and went to Rita.

"Girl, I in big trouble. Big, big trouble. If you know what Tiger go and do! He go and invite two Americans he does work with to come for Indian food tonight!"

"Is wat happen to him at all? He crack? He is ah damn fool in truth. He bringing wite people to eat in dat hut? Tiger must be really going out of he head, yes. Gul, yuh making joke!"

"Man, Rita, I tell you is true! My head hot! I don't know what to do."

"Well, yes," Rita mused, "Ah did know he chupid, but not so chupid! Well, all you have to do is do yuh best, gul."

"Rita, you go have to help me, girl."

"But sure, man. Wat yuh want me to do?"

"You have to lend me plenty thing. I want glass. Plate. Cup. Spoon. Knife. Fork. Tablecloth—"

"Take ease, keep cool! Between de two ah we we go fix up everyting good. Don't look so frighten. Why de hell yuh fraid Tiger so? Allyuh Indian people have some funny ways, *oui*."

"Girl, me and Tiger not like you and Joe. It different with we. If Tiger not pleased this evening, I sure he go beat me and kick me up. You don't know how funny he is these days. Last night he using one set of big words, I can't understand him at all."

"Well, look, Ah don't like how yuh getting so upset dese days, especially as de baby coming. You don't worry bout nutting, Ah go help yuh to do everyting."

On Rita's dumbwaiter were cutlery and glasses and a lot of table necessities which she used only at Christmas time. She cast a glance at them.

"Ah don't know why Ah doing dis," she grumbled. "Tiger is ah damn fool, and Joe tell me to keep from interfering in allyuh business. Allyuh not even creole like we. It look like if Ah always doing someting for you all. Ah always helping allyuh out ah someting."

Urmilla didn't know what to say.

Rita said, "Well, don't stand up dere like ah statue! Yuh ain't have nutting else to do?"

"I have to go and buy clothes for me and Chandra."

"Well, wat de hell yuh waiting for? Gone nar, yuh know how de morning does fly. By de time yuh come back Ah have everyting clean and wash, ready for yuh."

"I don't know what to tell you—"

"Gone, nar! Make haste and come back!"

She took Chandra in her arms and went to San Juan. She bought the clothes and a pair of sandals. The shoes felt strange on her feet; it was the first pair she had ever worn. She had imagined that when that time came it would be different, that by then they would have had their own house and she would go shopping like a lady, buying all the latest fashions. She was too excited to admire herself in the new sari, and the sandals pinched her feet; she took them off as soon as she got back home, washing the dirt off the soles.

Then she went to Tall Boy and bought everything she needed. Flour. Rice. Tiger hadn't said to buy rum, but he had also suggested that she should know what to buy. Tall Boy showed her the brand Tiger usually drank.

"That is the best rum you have, Tall Boy? You not have a better brand? I want the best you have."

"A-a, like allyuh having a party or wat?"

"Never mind, I want the best."

Tall Boy leaned over the counter. "Yuh getting nice dese days," he said, smiling and trying to touch her as she backed away. "Yuh cheeks getting rosy like mango, yuh breasts standing up nice! Ah next baby coming, eh?"

Urmilla blushed. "Man, Tall Boy, I ain't have time today with you! I in a hurry, man. Bring the rum."

He climbed up on a barrel and reached down a bottle from the top shelf. He wiped off the dust with a rag.

"De best rum. Olive Blossom. Barbados rum. Look ah map of Barbados on de label. Is de most expensive too. But ah never see Tiger drinking dis rum, yuh know. He does always drink Vat Nineteen."

"Don't mind. Is two bottles I want, man, not one!"

"Someting really happening home by you! Invite me to de party, nar?"

"Hurry up, man. Look other people in the shop who want message."

"Dis is ah big bill, Ah hope yuh paying cash, is about twelve dollar now. Yuh want anyting else? How about some cokes and some soda, to drink de rum? And some ice? If yuh wait till later all de ice might sell out. Ah will put away piece for you."

Urmilla paid him and hurried off to Deen's hut in tenth street. She wasn't friendly with them, but they had the best fowls in the village. Besides, Tiger had said to buy from them. If she didn't and something went wrong with the dinner and Tiger got to find out, he would say it was because she hadn't done as he ordered.

"Deen wife!" she called out.

"Who dat dere? Dat Tiger wife? Wat yuh want?"

"I want to buy two fowl. Two big fat one."

"We not have any fowl to sell yuh."

"But how, you have plenty, man! I ain't begging, you know, and I don't want you to trust me. I paying you you money right away."

Deen's wife said, "Is ah dollar ah pound if yuh want."

"What! Everybody else selling for three shillings a pound. You robbing me, man."

"Dese fowls we have here is de best in de village. Yuh forget everyting gone up since de war. Yuh know how much we does pay for chicken feed and mash? If yuh don't want to pay, go someway else. You and Tiger too cheap!"

Urmilla raised her hands and showed money. "Don't mind you robbing me, I will still buy, to show you we not cheap. Pick out two big fat one—I don't want any cock, give me two hen. And come quick, let we go in the shop and weigh it."

"We have scale right here. Look dese two. Let me see." Deen's wife tied the feet of the chickens together and tossed them on the scales. "Six pounds. Dat is six dollars."

"They don't feel heavy like six pounds."

"Well, go someway else."

"All right, all right, I ain't have time to argue, man. Look you money."

Deen's wife folded the bills small and pushed them in her bosom. "Like allyuh having ah big fete home by you," she observed as Urmilla left the yard.

By noon everyone in the village knew that something was happening home by Tiger because Urmilla had bought two bottles of Barbados rum and two fowls from Deen.

Urmilla knelt on the floor of the small kitchen and crushed the *tumric* and *dhania* with the massala stone.

Rita said, "If yuh want, yuh cud come over and use my stove to cook wid. It better dan dat mud fireplace yuh have, burning wood."

"No, girl!" Urmilla replied. "The best fire to cook with is wood fire, that is one thing I learn from the time I small. You can't cook roti and thing on stove."

All day she was in the kitchen, smelling the pot, tasting, giving Rita to taste. "How that taste, Rita? Is a good curry? You sure? It want more salt?"

"Don't fraid, gul. Yuh cook ah master food here. It go make dem Americans wish for more."

"I hope so. If anything go wrong, is better I dead!"

Rita was as anxious as Urmilla. She arranged the table. She put a bowl with hibiscus flowers and kept casting her eyes about the room, looking for something to do, to change. She couldn't do anything about the hut itself, except clean it out. The lamp should be placed on the table. But even with the wick turned right up, the light would still be dim. They should have another lamp.

Suddenly she said, "Ah-ha! Ah know wat Ah go do!" and she went to look for an extension cord Joe had brought home from the base. "Ah find it," was what he told her when she asked him how he got it. She fitted the cord in the socket in the dining room and passed it through the window.

"Ma, wat yuh doing?" Henry asked. He had just come home from school for lunch. He always called Rita "Ma" and had got to accepting her and Joe as his parents.

"Come, go outside and take de cord and pass it through de fence into Mr. Tiger house."

Henry did as he was told. Rita passed the cord in the window of the hut and screwed in a bulb.

"What you doing, girl?" Urmilla called from the kitchen.

"Come and yuh go see!" Rita put on the light. "Sun shining plenty, yuh can't see it good now, but wen it get dark yuh go have electric light. Yuh cud keep de lamp in de kitchen while yuh hotting over de food."

"Well, girl, I believe you would even give me your house and all!" Urmilla exclaimed. "Rita, you too good."

The dying sun reddened the sky and evening shadows fell. It was time to dress. To put on the new sari, standing in front of Rita's mirror and seeing how she looked. And the sandals.

"Don't do as if yuh never wear shoes in yuh life before," Rita said. "Walk as usually, don't bend up yuh foot so!"

"It have me uncomfortable, man." But she admired herself in the mirror, her wavy black hair falling down her back, the sari draped across her shoulders.

"I look good, Rita?"

"Gul, Tiger will fall all over for yuh again! But wait nar, yuh want some powder and rouge and lipstick—"

"What! No, girl, we Indian people don't put on that! You must be want Tiger to beat me up!"

"Don't talk damn foolishness! Yuh don't want to look good? No harm in dat. It ain't as if yuh putting it on every day, is just for de occasion. Try some, man, he wud be surprise."

"Well, just a little bit, but I really fraid, if Tiger—"

"To hell wid Tiger. Here, let me put it on for yuh. Hold steady, how yuh trembling so? Now, press yuh lip together, dat's right. Now look at yuhself in de glass."

Urmilla looked. It was pretty.

"That nough. Don't put any more."

"Put some rouge now, man." Rita rubbed her cheeks with the puff. "Now, ah little bit ah powder, just little bit. Stand off and let me see yuh. Oh gawd, yuh like craft fadder now! Is now yuh pretty, gul. Look at yuhself in de glass."

"My humble abode is not a massive structure," Tiger said as the jeep bumped along the street, "but I going to construct a building as soon as financial embarrassment over."

Chief laughed. He was sitting in the back with Tiger, and Larry was driving.

"It's the food we want to eat, John," chief said, "we've

heard so much about the Indian dishes in Trinidad that we thought we'd taste some, and the best place would be at an Indian home."

"My wife could really cook good," Tiger said, "your mouth will run water—I mean"—he swallowed—"your salivary glands will run when you eat that food."

"How long've you been living here, John?"

"Oh, since I get married."

"And the hut you live in, you built it yourself?"

"No, chief, I get it when I married. You see, is like this. When Indian people married, the man does have to start eating at the feast. Before that, everybody bring gifts—the guests and them. Then when the man feel he get sufficient, he start to eat. Is only then that the guests and them stop offering gifts."

"Hear that, Larry? And you didn't begin to eat until you'd got a lot, John?"

Tiger shook his head. "I was small, just a juvenile, and stupid then. My father did well vex up with me afterwards, he say I should have waited for more things before eating. But you know how it is when you small and stupid, chief! Sometimes I does think that if I did, am, hesitated more, like would have been different. I would have get plenty more things. But is only when you mature you does reflect of all that!"

"I'm .very interested in your customs, John. I understand that some Indians eat with their fingers. We want to do that too. We'd like everything to be as it always is. Hope you've not gone and made special preparations."

Larry drove the jeep off the road and stopped in the scrubby grass. "Well, here we are," he said, "and, boy, am I hungry! Bring out the Oriental dishes, John, and let us feast like gods!"

"It have plenty light in the house," Tiger observed. "I didn't know our lamp have so much appearance of brightness!"

He stopped short in the doorway and looked around the hut.

The table was laid with white linen. The silver cutlery and glasses sparkled in the light, emphasized by the drabness of the hut itself. Amber glowed from the two bottles of rum in a waiter, surrounded by small glasses and bottles of Coca-Cola. The electric light hung from the roof against the wall in a way as if it had always been there. Chandra, in a pink dress, rocked in the hammock in the corner, watching the strangers who had come inside.

"Well, make yourselves at home," Tiger said slowly, blinking his eyes and waving his hand towards Joe's cushioned chairs, "my wife must be in the kitchen."

Trembling. She had heard them come in and ran into the kitchen, her heart pounding with fear and excitement, not knowing what to do, whether she should be there to welcome them or with the baby or what. Rita had said don't be excited, just act natural, but she couldn't.

"Urmilla!" Tiger called, and she heard his voice as if a field of cane separated them, and the sound drifted away into the depths of the land.

"Urmilla, where you, in the kitchen? Come on, we reach."

And she put her sari on and hung her head and went and wouldn't lift her face.

"What do you know, she's shy," Larry said. "No need to be. John told us all about you."

And chief shook her hand, and Larry said, "That's a swell baby you have!" And she knew she had to say something or else Tiger would beat her, so she said, "No, sir, she not swell, is just that she getting fat."

Chief and Larry laughed and sat down.

Tiger said, "But what it is you do? You look different tonight. Let me look at you good, girl. Oh-ho! But—" He checked himself. It would have to be later, nothing must go wrong now.

Urmilla saw the look on his face and scurried to the kitchen with a murmured excuse. She hadn't been able to see if he was pleased or not, the look on his face was just one of amazement.

"What about a drink, chief?" Everything had to be later, after his bosses were gone, and he and Urmilla were alone. "This is the best rum in the West Indies, chief," he said. "It distilled in Barbados. It even better than we Trinidad rum!"

The Americans mixed their drinks with Coca-Cola, and Tiger followed them.

"Well, John, you sure have everything fixed up nicely here, you look cozy," chief observed. "Later on, where are you going to put up your massive structure, on this same site?"

"It hard to plan for the future right now," Tiger said, thinking of more things than one, and squatting on the floor.

"Hey!" Larry cried, "I thought there was something funny here. We should be squatting on the floor, in true Indian fashion!" and he slipped out of Joe's chair and joined Tiger.

Chief brought the waiter and glasses and put the bottle of rum down on the floor in front of them. "This is better," he said. "What about the wife, John, doesn't she fire one too?"

"No, chief, my wife doesn't drink at all!" he replied quickly.

"Oh, come on," Larry said, "let her have one with us. I'll go get her—you don't get up."

Something was wrong, he could sense it. He wanted to put it right, whatever it was. These natives had funny ways sometimes. You could never tell. You had to be careful with them.

"Come on in with us," Larry urged Urmilla, "come and have a drink with us, please."

She hung her head so he couldn't see her face. She shook her head. "I doesn't drink, sir."

"Oh, come on. Just one little one, huh? You want us to feel at home, don't you?"

She nodded.

"Well then, come on. We'll only feel at home if you do just as you always do when we're not here."

"Tiger say to come?"

"Yes. Don't be afraid of us. We're harmless, you'll see!" He spoke reassuringly.

Urmilla sat down in a chair.

"Down here, on the ground with us." Larry patted the floor and moved up. "That's better. You pour one for the wife, John, you know her capacity!"

Tiger didn't look at Urmilla as they drank. She had one and it steadied her somewhat.

"You've got a hard-working husband here," chief told her. "He's heading for promotion."

"I'd work hard too if I had as pretty a wife as you!" Larry said, and she blushed. She felt a little better. They were just ordinary people, after all. And the rum was getting them in a merry mood, even Tiger. Perhaps things might work out after all. Rita should see her now, sitting down on the floor with the Americans and laughing and talking!

"You know what, John," chief said, pouring more Coca-Cola in his glass, "I'm going to see that you get a promotion. We've finished with most of the surveying now, and next week we'll probably start laying boulders and gravel. How'd you like to check trucks?"

"Sure, chief, but I wouldn't like to stop working with you."

"Oh, never mind that! It's a better job, and you'll make more money. You want to make money, don't you? You leave it to me, I'll fix things up for you."

"Thanks a lot, chief. That will be my first work reading and writing."

"How come you have such a funny name, John? Why did they call you Tiger?"

"I don't know, I must be resemble a tiger! All my other brothers and sisters have good Indian nominations, is only me they give a funny name. But I never worry about it."

"But what's your surname, John? Your father's name?"

"Oh, he was name Baboolal. You know, we Indian people does call we father *bap* and we mother *mai*. Look, chief, when you all hungry just say the word, you know."

"Let's finish this bottle first. This sure is some rum. I must remember the brand."

Urmilla went to heat the food, thinking that if they all enjoyed it Tiger would be pleased. Already he was looking happy with the news of his promotion as a checker. So it was really a good thing that he learned to read and write!

When the bottle was finished and they broke the seal of the other, Urmilla brought in the food. Steaming white rice and savoury curry. Larry wanted to eat with his hands, but chief nudged him and whispered that it would look bad after all the preparations, so they sat down round the table.

Tiger said, "No formality, chief. Eat your belly full, plenty more food outside." And he fingered the knife and fork, which he was about to use for the first time in his life. He was waiting to see what the Americans would do, and then follow them.

Urmilla had retired to the kitchen to eat her food there, sitting on a box.

"Where's Urmilla, John? Isn't she joining us?" Larry asked.

"Is custom with we Indian people, when guests here the wife eat in the kitchen."

"Let me tell you something about customs, John"—Larry leaned over the table and wagged a knife in Tiger's face— "most of it is just plain dumb. A man hasn't got to live like that, John. A man must choose what he should do and what he shouldn't do, not be forced into anything just because it is a custom or a tradition. You mustn't let things rule you, John, you must rule things."

"Well, to tell you the truth, Mr. Larry, I never pay much attention to them things. I does figure out things for myself, and do what I feel is the right thing."

"That's right. You see, it's like this. You really feel Urmilla should be here with us, huh? Look, there's plenty room here between us. I'll go get her."

"Well, is all right if she want to come."

She had already begun to eat, one hand was in the food. She blushed when she saw him. But the rum had made him gay and he drowned her protests and led her to the table.

"Here, we'll do it this way, as if we're having a big party. John, pour out the drinks—plenty of Cokes for me. And no knives and forks!"

"Okay then," chief agreed, laughing, "we'll all eat with our fingers. This'll be something to write the folks about!"

"You sure, chief? Don't inconvenience yourself because of Urmilla and me, you know."

Larry laughed. "Why, I'm now beginning to enjoy it! Here, Urmilla, you show me how."

Urmilla hung her head. Not only Tiger but her parents would quarrel if they saw her sitting at table like that with her husband's guests. She trembled inwardly and didn't look at Tiger. Perhaps she had shamed him, she didn't know. She only knew she had tried so hard to do everything right.

They all ate heartily, their appetites roused by the rum. And every few minutes Larry would pass around the bottle. Tiger seemed to be getting in a good mood; by the time she cleared away the dirty dishes and plates she knew for sure that at least nothing was wrong with the food.

They sat down, smoking and talking afterwards, not taking

quick short drinks again, but filling up their glasses with Cokes and little rum, and sipping.

"Quiet around here, John," chief said. "Nice area to live in. Something about Trinidad gets me, Larry. I don't know what it is, if it's the air or the land or the people or the sun in the sky all day long."

"Gets me too," Larry murmured, leaning back and sipping slowly at his drink. "Funny, I never thought it would be like this. I expected hula-hula girls in grass skirts, and natives creeping through the bush with bows and arrows! Instead, what do I see? A modern city streaming with American cars, people dressed to kill in the latest fashions."

"Well," chief said, "when I heard I was drafted to a West Indian island called Trinidad, I thought it was the last outpost, believe me. I'd never heard of it—I know Jamaica, because we heard about it, and once me and the gal thought of spending a long holiday there." He sighed. "Anyway, now that I've seen Trinidad, I think we'll come here instead. I was really surprised too. It's a fascinating place, but besides that, the people are up-to-date on everything, and keeping abreast of the times too." He turned to Tiger. "How is your government run, John?"

"Well, chief," Tiger said, thinking hard, "I not too sure. I don't pay much attention to politics and thing."

"It's politics that builds a country, John, don't ever forget that. Don't sit back and let things happen to you. Interest yourself in how you are governed, find out why laws are passed. Oh yes, I've already seen you're an easygoing people. But, John, when you vote for a man who gets a seat on the government, remember that you want a man there who'd fight for your rights, a man you and other poor people like you could trust, a man who—what the hell am I talking politics for, anyway!"

"Is politics that build a country, chief," Tiger repeated.

"Yeah. Sure." He looked at Larry. "You seem to be damn comfortable, but we gotta be going."

"If you had a guitar," Larry said, "and could sing us some calypsoes—" He rose and stretched. "John, this is just about the best food I've tasted since I left home. Boy, can your wife cook!"

They shook hands with Tiger, and Larry went to the kitchen for the third time and said, "So long, beautiful. Tuck John in, he appears to be somewhat tight, not—hic—that I'm so sober myself!"

Joe Martin surveyed the room and exploded. "Ah tell yuh already, keep out of dem coolie people business! Wat de arse yuh have to interfere wid dem for? Look, Ah going and out de damn light, man. If Tiger want electric light in 'e house, 'e cud pay for it, he working for plenty money now."

"You haul yuh tail!" Rita flared. "Dey is my friends, and I lend dem dose tings. Wat yuh making noise for? Yuh fraid yuh wares get break up? De man must make impression on he boss. You ain't even have dat ambition, so long yuh working in de base, yuh never bring an American home, to eat good creole food, calallo, peas, rice—"

"Wat de arse yuh tink, I running ah boarding house? Yuh too damn soft. Dat Indian girl only have to come and say, 'Rit—a—a, lend me ah pot, ple—a—s—e—e—,' and yuh gone mad, yuh giving she everyting it have in de house. Yuh won't like to move over in de hut, and let dem come and live in dis house, eh? Ah don't understand dat damn fool Tiger. He buying brick to build house, and he ain't even have furniture yet. He planning to lick down de hut and build house, and he wife ain't even have clothes to wear or shoes to put on. All of dat is damn slackness, man. Why de arse yuh have to drag me in it? Ah suppose yuh lend she ah dress to put on too?"

"Yuh ain't have no compassion! Look at yuh, yuh cud see yuh come from George Street! Yuh don't know nutting bout friend or neighbour or helping oder people—"

"To arse wid dat! Nobody ever help me. I catch me royal from de time Ah small, living de hard way. Yuh won't say Tiger ever do anyting for me! Way he know how to eat wid knife and fork? Yuh don't know coolie people does eat wid dey hand? Man, look, Ah telling yuh, dis is de last time yuh get on wid dis slackness, yuh hear, if anyting so happen again, I beat yuh like ah snake!"

"Beat who like ah snake? But look at he, nar! Man, go and drown yuhself!"

"Look, Rita!" Joe advanced menacingly. "Ah see Ah go have to beat yuh tonight. Yuh getting too out ah hand. Take dat, and dat!"

"Oh—ho, yuh want to fight! Just let me take off dis high heel shoes and see if Ah don't bust in on yuh head!"

She struggled with Joe.

Tiger said, "You look like a whore in Port of Spain, with all that thing on your face. You shame me. Is which part you get all those things? Don't tell me! I know! Is Rita! She who give you lipstick and thing to put on too, eh?"

"Oh God, Tiger, I did think you would please, but I too sorry. Is I who put it on for myself, thinking you would like it. She didn't give me, she advise me not to use it."

"And all them plate glass and knife and fork? Is she who give you? You don't know we have money and could buy things for weself?"

"You does always say so, but you don't never buy anything."

"Oh—ho, you giving back answers too! You getting on preposterous! You getting on a high horse, you playing indignant!

You nev,er taste the weight of my foot, girl. Is time. I go learn you respect. I go learn you who is man in this house."

Urmilla cowered. "Oh God, I beg you pardon," she sobbed and clasped her hands to her bosom.

"Take that!" He kicked her across the face. "And that!" He kicked her in her stomach, and she doubled up in agony. He kicked her as she writhed on the floor, the rum spinning in his head and making him dizzy. And when he was tired he looked around for something else to kick, and the electric light danced in his brain. He jumped to reach it to tear it down but missed and fell, his knees buckling.

He lay on the ground, snoring loudly and rolling in a deep sleep.

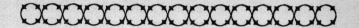

CHAPTER TEN

The cost of living rose in 1943 from 177 points to 194, and an old Negro woman, purporting to be a seer and dressed as one, stood in front of a court in St. Vincent Street and bawled out that the world was coming to an end and the first building to fall would be the Red House. A young Chinese journalist looking for a human story saw her and wrote a report; her picture appeared in the *Evening News*. Imported foodstuffs were reduced to the barest minimum, entertainment was taxed, transport facilities curtailed, shopping hours shortened, and earnest consideration given to the introduction of rationing. A coloured girl fainted in Frederick Street one day, worrying because she had an American soldier friend and hadn't seen her time for the month. The campaign to grow more food was intensified. Cane farmers especially were called upon to safeguard the future of the industry by pressing forward with their planting, thus also providing work for the populace when construction of the United States bases ceased. The Education Board approved new scales of salaries for teachers. A rent restriction bill was passed, but people who urgently wanted houses didn't mind paying what ruthless owners asked; those who cooperated found themselves hounded by the owners until they had to leave. The Governor went to London and came back and said he had found a greatly increased interest in the colonies and in colonial affairs, and some people put their hands to their mouths and smiled. In La Brea, south of the island, a man walking through the fields from work late at night fled in terror when he saw a giant donkey, "bout twenty thirty feet high," appear out of the darkness. Another report from a lonely district was that a man and his wife had stumbled over a coffin in the centre of a darkened road. A man appeared in court for murder, having chopped off his wife's head with a cutlass. As the Caribbean was fraught with peril on account of submarines, the government agreed to accept responsibility for loss by enemy action of cargoes shipped to and from Barbados, two hundred miles away. A new Colonial Secretary arrived, and the island was host to five Venezuelan cabinet ministers and their wives during an official visit.

The road rapidly advanced. Boulders and gravel from the Laventille Quarry and other sites were brought in by trucks. Where the land was soft stones were laid two feet deep. Then gravel stones consisting chiefly of different kinds of quartz, obtained from river beds in the Northern Range, were laid. Military traffic was allowed to run on this surface to level it out. When defective spots showed up the work had to be done all over again, giving a completely new foundation.

The rainy season came. Rain lashed the earth and flooded the rivers, carrying away crops and livestock. The sun would shine brilliantly in the morning, but by midday hovering clouds would mass and it rained heavily for hours, sometimes through the night and the following day.

Tiger got up one night. Two things woke him. The roof was leaking, and he was wet. And his wife was groaning. He ignored the leak.

"Urmilla," he whispered, shaking her, "you sick bad? You want me to go for a doctor?"

The girl moaned. She had been sick for weeks, growing worse. Pains all over her body. She had fever.

"Give me some of the medicine you get from the drugstore," she said, gasping.

"But these nights like you getting worse, really, I think I going for a doctor."

He was frightened for himself. Everything had been going wrong, though he was making plenty money. And if that was happening, it was only himself to blame. It had started out all right, until the night he brought the chief and Mr. Larry home. Then after that a blur came before his eyes and it wouldn't go, no matter how much he rubbed them or shook his head. A sort of haze, as if he couldn't see properly. Joe and Rita were not talking to him, though they came to see Urmilla. They acted as if he wasn't there at all, and he felt a burning shame, but he was too proud to let them see. He ignored them too. Whenever they came he left, walking in the rain, rubbing his eyes. He went by Boysie and played cards. Or he went to San Juan to see a film. Or he just stayed out, alone in the night, walking until he was not aware of motion, arguing with himself. He didn't want to drink, but sometimes with nothing else to do he found himself in the rumshop. And the next he knew he was drunk. Once Joe pulled him up. Joe said, "Wat happening to yuh? Yuh can't see yuh wife sick bad? Yuh getting on like ah little boy still. If I was yuh fadder Ah beat yuh till yuh can't stand up." "Mind yuh own business!" he had snarled back, "I capable of managing my own affairs." But Joe had scared him; he went to the drugstore and bought some medicine.

Still, it looked like Urmilla wasn't getting any better. Coughing and choking in the night, fighting to breathe. He didn't know what to tell her when he lay next to her. He only rolled and tossed in his sleep and ground his teeth. Even the road had lost interest for him, though the work had progressed and it was in shape, a level stretch winding down behind the village. Even the job was distasteful, and one day he had told the foreman, "Look, I don't want to do this checking work no more. Put me back with the working gang, let me do hard work." And he went back smashing boulders and pounding into the land, and rain washed his perspiration away, and still he worked, day after day, thinking that he would get so tired he wouldn't lay awake in the night and hear Urmilla groaning. He learned to drive a bulldozer because he wanted to hurl it against the land and the trees; when he sat down in the seat he felt the power beneath him, and he dug up the land and crushed the bushes and wished it had more speed, so he could smash into a tree and hear the sound of the impact, and how the fibres in the trunk tore apart. But one week of this and he realized that it was the bulldozer and not himself who was doing the work, and he went back with the road gang again, and the foreman said that if he wanted a next transfer he could haul his tail right back home.

He got up and dressed. "Urmilla," he whispered, "I going to get a doctor. I can't bear to see you suffering so, man. Don't fraid to stay alone, I go come back quick."

"Tiger, ask Rita to stay with me till you come back?"

"It too late, man! They must be gone to sleep already. I won't stay long, I go take taxi to go and come."

He went out, pulling an old felt hat over his head. The yard was flooded with muddy water, and the rose mango tree shook heavy drops onto the roof when the wind blew. He shivered a little and kept his eyes wide open for holes of mud in the road. When the rainy season started the estate people had sent trucks with a kind of loose, red gravel to fill the holes. But these were only muddy pools now. Progress was too slow watching out for the holes in the darkened streets, so he walked on the grass at the side.

The night was deserted. He stood by the main road for five minutes before he was able to stop a taxi. He asked the driver if he knew where a doctor was living.

"Which doctor?"

"Any one, man. My wife sick bad, and I have to get one right away. Do quick."

"So wat about de passenger Ah have in de back?"

The passenger, a young man from the city who had attended a Dutch party in San Juan, got out.

"Is all right, pal. I would catch another taxi."

"Thanks, man," Tiger said and got in.

"Dey have ah doctor in San Juan," the driver said, reversing in sixth avenue, "is ah Indian doctor, living Santa Cruz Old Road. Let we try dere first."

The wheels squelched on the wet asphalt, and the headlights cut across lances of rain.

Tiger got out and pounded at the door. It was after midnight, and the wind rustled through the trees and drops of water fell with a distinct sound apart from the rain, keeping up a monotonous patter on the galvanized roofs.

After what seemed to him hours of waiting a light went on and a cautious voice called, "Who is there?"

"Is me, doctor," Tiger shouted, "my wife sick too bad."

"Who is it?"

"A man from Barataria, doctor, you don't know me."

"Well, what do you expect me to do? What's wrong with her, man?"

"I don't know, doctor, that is why I come. But she sick bad. Do quick, please, doctor. I will pay you good—"

"Give me your address"—the voice still came from inside—
"I'll come in the morning and see her."

"But is now she sick, doctor—"

"Oh, come back in the morning, man. Rain falling. It must
be just a belly ache. Give her some pot soda to drink."

And the light went out.

"But—" Tiger looked at the windows. "This is a hell of a
thing," he said to the driver. "I can't understand this thing at
all. You sure is a Indian doctor?"

"But how yuh mean if Ah sure? I living in San Juan from
de time Ah small, yuh go ask me if Ah sure! Ah must know.
It look like you outta luck. Let we try someway else, den. It
have ah creole doctor in Laventille."

"But I still can't understand this kind of thing," Tiger kept
saying as the car drove through the rain. "Ain't he is a
doctor?"

"Is so wen yuh poor and not in society, papa," the driver
said. "Boy, if I tell yuh about some of de doctors in dis place,
yuh dead."

"But who say I poor? I was going to pay him, anything he
ask for."

"Still, look at yuh. He must be peep from de window and
see ah coolie boy standing up dere pounding he door. Yuh tink
dem doctor go leave dey bed to go and look at any poor sick
coolie woman dis hour of de night? Yuh crazy!"

"Well, it might be worse if this man here is a creole doctor."

"Go try, man," the driver said, stopping in front of the house
on the main road.

Tiger bawled out, "Good night, doctor! Good night!"

Again a light went on. Again a voice said, "Who is that?"
Only the voice was arrogant this time.

"Is a man from Barataria, doctor. My wife sick too bad, I

frighten. You could come now, please? I have a car waiting here, we could go back right away—"

"Are you a patient of mine? Have I ever attended to you or your wife before? Who is your regular doctor?"

"No, doctor, but please come quick, she sick too bad."

"I'm afraid you'll have to come back in the morning, my good man. It's only a few hours more, she won't die."

And the light went out.

"But this is a hell of a country!" Tiger exclaimed. "You mean I can't get a doctor to come and see my wife just because is night and rain falling?"

"We cud try Port of Spain," the driver said, "but Ah only hope yuh paying me good for dis job! But dere might be worse, yuh know, as is only big-shot wite doctor dat Ah know. Anyway"—he reckoned his increasing fare—"come go, Ah know ah good doctor in St. Clair."

"This time I go be lucky," Tiger said, getting out in the rain. "Look, he have a brass sign on the door here, saying he is a doctor."

There was a bell hanging near the door, and he rang it loudly and waited, lighting a cigarette and throwing the pack to the driver.

This time someone came to the door. It was the doctor himself, a white man, with a robe pulled on hurriedly over his pajamas.

"Yes, what is it?" he asked, then added, "Come in out of the rain."

Tiger stammered, "Sir, my wife sick too bad. I fraid something might happen. You could come?"

"Where do you live?" the doctor asked.

"In Barataria, sir. Not too far from here. Don't mind if I looking poor, sir. I have plenty money to pay, and a car waiting outside, to bring you back too. Don't mind I not in your society, sir. I try two other doctor, and they say to wait till morning. But she sick bad, sir. A long time, but like she take in worse tonight—"

"All right, all right. Give me a few minutes to get dressed. You could send the taxi away, we'll go in my car. Do you know exactly what's wrong?"

Tiger hesitated. "No, sir, but she have plenty pains—"

"Pregnant?"

"What you say, sir?"

"Is she going to have a baby?"

"Oh, not now, sir. Plenty time yet."

The doctor hurried inside, and Tiger went out to the driver and paid him.

"Well, look at dat, eh boy! Yuh own people let yuh down, and is ah wite man who going to see yuh wife. Well, yes!"

"I will never forget tonight, boy," Tiger told him and watched the taxi drive off, thinking bitterly.

"Don't be too worried," the doctor said, "she's probably going to have her baby before her time. It happens to many people."

The car turned off the main road into the village.

"Mind the roads, sir," Tiger said, "it have plenty holes."

"I've heard about it."

Tiger lit the lamp and stood by the doctor. He was kneeling on the floor, feeling her pulse.

"How do you feel, girl?" he asked kindly, and Urmilla groaned and pointed to her stomach.

"How long have you been preg—how long since you knew you were going to have a child?"

"About six months, doctor," she whispered.

"Hmm." He got up and addressed Tiger.

"Your wife's very ill," he said, "you'll have to be very careful with her. She's very weak and mustn't do a stroke of work, you understand? And let her keep in bed, very quiet. Nothing must disturb her."

He looked at Chandra sleeping in the hammock. "Who delivered the first child?"

"My neighbour, sir. A creole woman name Rita."

The doctor nodded slowly. "I am going to give you a prescription. See that she takes the medicine regularly. And it may be as well if you let a professional doctor or a midwife attend to her when her time comes. It may be complicated, something may happen which your neighbour doesn't understand anything about. You follow?"

Tiger nodded. "Is all right, sir? Nothing wrong with she?"

"How do you mean nothing's wrong with her? My dear man, if she gets out of bed and exerts herself, it may be fatal. It's up to you to care for her. Nothing more I can do."

"Doctor," Tiger said, "I don't know how to tell you how I 'preciate how you come. I thank you very much. Is how much I owe you, sir?"

"The fee's usually two dollars for visiting sick people, my boy."

"What! Only that, doctor? After you take all that trouble to leave your house in Port of Spain and come quite up here in the village?"

The doctor smiled and looked around the hut. He took a phial of pills from his case. "And these are two shillings—they'll help her to sleep."

"Doctor, if is anything you want any time, just tell me. I know how things hard to get now, but I will get the best for you, big tomatoes, fresh lettuce—you seeing any trouble to get meat in Port of Spain? I could fix up with our butcher here—"

"I manage all right, but thank you all the same."

"Look, it have some tomatoes here still. I grow them myself. Take some, doctor, two dollars is too little bit of money for all you trouble. You is a good man, doctor. You don't belong to this country? Where you come from, England?"

The doctor put on his hat and yawned. "Yes—wish I was back there now. Ah well." He stretched and said good night, and Tiger went out in the rain with him and put the bag of tomatoes in the back seat.

He gave Urmilla one of the tablets and she dropped off into a deep sleep.

He lay there smoking and thinking.

He didn't go to work the next day. He went in search of the Indian doctor in San Juan. When he found the place he told the nurse, a middle-class Indian girl, that he wanted to see the doctor.

"You have to wait," she said, pointing to the patients who were sitting in chairs, looking at magazines.

He sat down, then he got up and paced the floor, to keep moving.

The door behind the nurse opened and the doctor appeared, holding on to the knob.

"Who's next, please?" he called in a pleasant voice.

"Is I next, but I don't have to go inside, I could tell you what I have to say right here," Tiger shouted, and he swallowed hard for the words to come. "It have a lot of you people who have money, and big profession, and have car and moving in high society, but for all that all you ain't have no mind! All you only playing doctor! But all you don't even know what the word mean! All you don't have pity, all you don't know what it is to suffer!"

"Who is this man?" The doctor turned his head to the nurse.

"I don't know. He just come in—"

"Who is this man! Hear him! Who is this man! Is the man who come last night, begging you to go and see he wife who sick bad, and you turn out the light in my face! That is who it is! But a day will come when all you can't treat people like that!" Tears came to his eyes and he choked. "That is all I have to tell you."

He walked out of the office, swinging his arms, and the patients stood up in their chairs, open-mouthed, and the doctor said, laughing uneasily, "He must be a madman! But we can't keep the people waiting. I don't suppose any of you happen to know him, or where he's from?"

Tiger found the taxi was travelling too slow, because he didn't want the anger in him to go away. He got off in Laventille.

The Negro doctor had just returned from a visit to a patient in Success Village, near the city. He turned up the windshields of the Baby Ford and put the switchkey in his pocket. Vagabonds in the district went about tampering with cars, and whenever he parked it he made sure the doors were locked and there was no way of getting inside.

"You call yourself a doctor!" Tiger cried.

"I beg your pardon?" the doctor asked in a cultured voice, slightly raising his eyebrows.

Tiger laughed bitterly. "I beg your pardon! You know all the pretty words, but I shame of all Trinidad doctor. You know what happen last night? Let me tell you. Don't go yet"—holding on to his arm—"you talking like a social man, well, you don't know is manners to listen when somebody talking to you? Let me tell you. First, I went to a coolie doctor. Yes, a coolie like myself. You know what he do? He out the light in my face. Then I come by you. You don't want me to tell you what you do! You know that for yourself! But you know who I get eventually? You know? You don't know? Is a wite man! Yes, a wite doctor from England, who don't even belong to this country! Is he who come, quite from Port of Spain, to see my wife. All you ain't shame? You own people you doing that to? And I say again, man, look who it is that come? A big wite man!"

"Look here, my good man—" the doctor began, tugging away his arm and eyeing the crowd Tiger's shouts had attracted.

"Don't use fancy phrase on me, man! Don't call me a good man, you don't even know me, so how you could know if I good? But at least I is a Trinidadian like yourself, and it was a wite man who had to come to poor Tiger hut to see he wife, while you and that other nasty coolie man who say he is a doctor too didn't want to come. Is night! Rain falling! What happen, eh? You must be thought I didn't have money to pay?" He pulled out a wad of bills from his pocket. "Look!" He wet his thumb with his tongue and flicked the notes. "Look, money. Plenty. Is not bad money, it as good as anybody else own."

The doctor eyed the crowd again and turned his back on Tiger and walked quickly up the steps of his office.

"Wat happen, pardner?"

"Wat it is? Somebody fighting?"

"Dat was de doctor yuh talking so to, boy, yuh brave!"

Tiger spun around. "Nothing much, man. Is just these damn people who have money and moving in society, who does laugh and spit on we poor people." He talked to the crowd. "Last night my wife was sick bad, you see, so I come in a taxi looking for a doctor. Two of them I try, the Indian one in San Juan and this one here. You know what they do? They tell me to come back tomorrow, and they out the light in my face! But the hurtful part, man, the part that hurt me most, is that I had to go quite in Port of Spain, in St. Clair, and who you think I get? A wite doctor, man! You don't see how is a shame? I mean, you don't see how wite man must always laugh at we coloured people, because we so stupid? You don't see why it is that black people can't get on in this country at all at all?"

The people murmured in agreement. A wrong done to one was a wrong done to all.

"Same ting happen wen my old queen was sick, no doctor won't come, we had was to wait till morning."

"Boy, yuh never hear ting yet! If Ah tell yuh bout de time wen—"

"Black people cud never rise in dis world!"

"Me daughter sick, but Ah won't send she by him!"

"But what we going to do about this thing, man?" Tiger cried. "How long this kind of thing going on? Why the people who ruling we don't do something about it? Why we weself don't do something about it?"

"Is true, is true!"

"Keep yuh mouth quiet, yuh know anyting bout it, yuh know wat we talking about?"

"Trinidadians does only talk, dey don't do nutting."

"He own people let him down! Yuh went and curse de coolie doctor too?"

The crowd dispersed slowly, arguing and gesticulating. It was a long time before they went about their business.

Every day it rained heavily, and weeds and grasses shot up in the air overnight, and there were many jobs for those who had cutlasses and hoes, going from house to house, cleaning the yards. Even in the drains grass grew, and estate labourers cleaned them, draining the stagnant water and banking the black mud at the sides to prevent mosquitoes breeding. The roads were in a muddy mess, so flooded at times as to be entirely impassable on foot. Only the farmers and the poorer people without shoes waded across the pools, and the children splashed in the water, and the ducks shook their tails and bathed.

Tiger worked far from home, in country districts where he made new friends. He worked ferociously, straining his body to the utmost. The sun never lasted long enough to dry the land, but it made no difference to him. He liked to work in the rain just as much as the sun. There were times when he came home so exhausted that he just dropped down and went to sleep right away.

All round, relationships were better. The past seemed to have been forgotten, and only the future mattered. Rita attended to Urmilla and cooked sometimes for him, though she avoided having any words with him. There was nothing he could do about it. He couldn't stay away from work now.

Joe met him in the shop and spoke casually, as if nothing had ever happened between them, but they never drank together. He knew what Joe was thinking about him.

The season of mangoes came, and the rose mango tree in the yard bloomed, and Tiger knew it was all going to happen again, another child, another night of thought. He didn't bother to pray for a boy child. He wasn't very enthusiastic. It didn't seem to matter whether it was a boy or a girl. What had to happen, had to happen.

But it mattered a great deal to Urmilla. Only a boy child could bring Tiger back to her as he used to be. A boy child would change him, they would be happy again as the first time, and the family would come from Chaguanas and they would celebrate. She knew it was going to be more painful this time, although Rita had said that after the first child it would be easier. But she wasn't feeling well. She was very sick. She used to imagine the pain, and fight against it, practising for when the time really came.

One night she said to Tiger, "Rita helping us a lot still, you know. She is a good woman."

Tiger pulled hard at his cigarette.

"Tiger, I want you to promise me one thing. If I plant you, you will grow?"

"Well, it depends. What it is?"

"You must let Rita deliver the baby, don't mind you vex with them."

"But, girl! Ain't I tell you what the doctor say? You have to have a doctor, man. He say it might be complicated. And you forget that Rita ain't no nurse—I mean, something might happen which she don't know bout."

"Tiger, I begging you. Rita know what she doing, I don't want no doctor. Rita like a mother to me."

"But, girl, this thing serious. The doctor know what he talking about. He is a big professional, and he tell me that is the best thing to do."

"If something to happen, I rather it happen with Rita than any doctor. Please, Tiger, I begging you, let she see bout me."

Rita broke the silence the next evening.

"Tiger, yuh know yuh wife want me to deliver she baby?"

Tiger nodded.

"Yuh know de doctor say she not well? Yuh know I not no midwife or nurse or anyting? Yuh don't want ah midwife to come and see she? It have one living just up de road, yuh know."

"What Urmilla say?"

"She say she want me alone, and nobody else. But yuh don't have to listen to wat she say, you have to make up yuh mind too. I ain't no doctor. Is true Ah deliver many children, but Ah want yuh to know in front dat Ah can't stand no responsibility for anyting dat happen. Joe telling me don't do dis ting, and Ah really going against me mind."

"Well, let we get a midwife, eh, Rita? Let we get somebody to examine she. What I must do? I don't know anything about that sort of thing." He flung his hands helplessly in the air.

"Well, go see de midwife. She name Miss Roberts, she living near de railway line, by eight avenue."

Miss Roberts, a middle-class, middle-aged coloured woman, had a sign on her gate, reading: "Registered Midwife." She promised to visit Urmilla the next day, and she did.

After the examination she said, "There is still a week or so to go. I have to be in town on another case for the rest of this week. If you want, you could take another midwife, and I won't charge you for this visit."

"But if it have time is all right, because you coming back from town next week. You don't think so, Rita?"

Rita looked doubtful and hesitated, but Urmilla said, "Is all right. And I have you, Rita?"

Tiger worked with his mind easier. Everything looked like it was going to come out all right. And from that day he began to pray for a boy child. Not too fervently. He prayed, "God, I want a boy child too bad, but if you send a girl, is all right. But a boy would make me happier."

It happened on a windy and raining night, earlier than they had expected, with the roof still leaking and the midwife in Port of Spain. The extension cord came through the window. Joe helped.

Rita asked Tiger, "Yuh have rum in de house? Pour ah good shot for me, Ah trembling."

Tiger was nervous too, he had one with her.

"You think I should go for a doctor, Rita? You sure is all right?"

She put down the glass and held his shoulders. "Look, Ah not sure about anyting tonight. Ah want yuh to know dat Ah will do my best, but Ah can't stand no responsibility. Yuh understand dat? Yuh sure yuh understand, Tiger?"

"Rita, it too late to go for a doctor?"

"Watch how late it is, and rain falling heavy. It ain't have time for dat now. Ah beginning to tink again dat Ah shudda keep out ah dis ting, yes. But it look as if I can't help dat now. Remember wat I tell yuh, boy. Don't blame me if it don't happen like how we want it."

He nodded and looked away outside, at the rain and the dark, feeling like a disaster was about to take place, and it was all his fault, everything that had happened, he was the cause of it.

He took Chandra sleeping in his arms and went over to Joe.

"Dis is ah helluva ting, boy," Joe said. "Yuh see how we come in allyuh business, though I warn Rita. Ah tell she to keep out ah allyuh affairs, now look wat go and happen. She ain't no nurse, she don't know ah damn ting about dis case. De doctor say yuh wife sick. Man, yuh shudda get ah doctor, man."

"Joe, you think I should go now? If I get a fast taxi, and we speed to town and get the same doctor that come last time, the one who—"

"Is only now yuh tinking bout dat? It too late now, man. We just have to wait and see wat go happen."

"This is a big thing for me, Joe—"

"Yuh start talking like dat again? Yuh remember de last time, how we sit down on de back step and fire, and eat mango, and how yuh did say den dat is ah big ting? It look to me like it go be de biggest ting."

"Joe, life is a funny thing, boy."

"Yes, it too f—— up."

"Joe, look how much thing happen to me since I come up

here to live. Look how we make friend, then we vex, then we make friend again. Joe, a man should hold on to what he have, you don't think so?"

"Eh—heh."

"And I mean, he should be glad for what he have, he shouldn't want too much thing. He shouldn't plan too much about the future, because he can't tell what going to happen. Not true, Joe?"

"Yuh now talking smart."

"And I mean, things like wife and children and a place to live, and some food in his belly, is enough for the time being. He shouldn't want to do big things right away, he should take time, he should wait for chances and opportunities. He should be grateful for what he have, don't mind it small. I mean, if you have something small, your neighbour does always have something smaller, so you see, you all right! You know, Joe, the main thing is to be happy, nothing else don't matter as long as you happy. But if even you could read and write, if even you have plenty money, big car, big house, big-shot friends, all of that don't matter if you not happy, not true, Joe?"

"Like yuh now starting to learn sense." Joe reached for a bottle of rum. "Let we fire one, Ah feeling dis ting just as much as yôu."

"Joe, you know Boysie say he going away after the war over. He say he going America. I ask him if he coming back, and he say he don't know. But I mean, this is a good country, Joe. Is only that we does let the government do we as they like, and we does put the wrong men in the legislature to demand we rights for we. You don't think so, Joe?"

"Eh—heh. Go on talking, yuh keeping me mind from tinking."

"And, Joe, ain't all of we does live good? Ain't coolie does live good with nigger? Is only wite man who want to keep we down, and even so it have some good one among them. You know something, Joe, they have good and bad all about, don't matter if you wite or black."

"Sure."

"Boy, one day I go become a politician. Is politics that build a country, you know that, Joe?"

"Why yuh don't tink bout going back to India?"

"What I would go back there for, Joe? I born in this country, Trinidad is my land. And the way how things shaping up, it look like a lot of things will be happening here. Boy, people not as stupid as long time. This country young, it have a long way to go—Joe, you think everything going all right? You don't find Rita staying a long time? Like I could hear Urmilla crying out hard."

"Fire one. Yuh was telling me about politics."

"Man, I don't know, man. Everything confuse in my mind. Joe, you know, is a funny thing, but I never grow up as Indian, you know—"

"Well, is bout three hundred time yuh tell me so already."

"I mean, it look to me as if everybody is the same. It have so many different kinds of people in Trinidad, boy! You think I should start to wear dhoti? Or I should dress as everybody else, and don't worry about Indian so much, but think of all of we as a whole, living in one country, fighting for we rights?"

"Man, Ah don't know about dat, nar. Ain't yuh is ah Trinidadian? Ain't yuh creolize? Wat yuh worrying bout?"

"Well, somebody have to worry, Joe. If we stay stupid and let things happen to we all the time, we go always stay so, poor and ignorant. That is the trouble with we, Joe. We does only talk, and we don't do anything. We does always say we must do this and do that, and we sit down on we tail and don't do nothing. Boy, I don't know, man. Everything really confuse in my mind, as if I can't think good. A fellar was telling me the other day that he would prefer to live under the Stars and Stripes than the British Bulldog. He say how much thing the Yankee do for this country since they come, look how much modern machinery they have, look how much more money they paying we."

"Don't worry wid he. He ain't tell yuh bout how dey does kick nigger over dere in America, and how dey does kill dem and shoot dem down like dog? He ain't tell yuh bout dat? Bout how dey have ah big notice in de road, saying: 'Nigger Keep Out.' He ain't tell yuh dat nigger does catch dey royal arse in de States? De Yankee dollar fooling ah lot ah dem. Boy, Ah don't like de British, but if it come to de worse, Ah radder stay wid dem any day dan live under American rule!"

"I hear that one time America did ask England to give she Trinidad."

"Is ah lucky ting dat didn't happen! It wudda been blood and sand in dis place, Ah tell yuh. Dey better haul dey tail out ah dis country quick, if dey know wat good for dem."

"But listen, it ain't have a way how we could govern weself? Ain't it have a thing call self-government?"

"Yes, Ah hear bout it. Dat is wat we fighting for now, but you yuhself know how dis place have so much different people, it go be ah big fight. Is always wite man for wite man, coolie for coolie, nigger for nigger."

"Boy, it have plenty small-island in Trinidad now. St. Lucian, Grenadian, Barbadian."

"Yuh know dey start long time to lay off people in de bases? Is like hell for all ah dem to find work now. De Yankee work finishing, so dey wud only have to go back way dey come from."

They lapsed into a short silence.

"Joe, I was thinking, we mustn't get vex again, you hear.

All you is good neighbours, and you is my best friend now
that Sookdeo dead and gone. We mustn't quarrel again."

"Yuh too damn cheap, yuh wife always borrowing someting
from Rita, why yuh don't buy yuh own tings?"

"I saving up money. I don't want to plan too much about
what I going to do, but things will change, Joe. We go have a
house just like you, and we won't have to borrow nothing."

Rita appeared suddenly in the doorway.

"Oh God, but you frighten me, Rita!" Tiger exclaimed,
leaping to his feet. "Is what happen? Everything all right? Is
a boy child?"

"Yes, Tiger, is ah boy child."

"Oh, I so glad! You hear, Joe? Is a boy! How Urmilla?"
He noticed the look on Rita's face. "Everything all right?"

"Urmilla all right, Tiger, but de baby born dead."

They used modern Barber Green equipment for the final
stages of the road. A supply depot was established on the route,
and trucks fed the machinery with gravel and asphalt. The
asphalt came from the famous Pitch Lake in La Brea, a southern district. The gravel and asphalt were mixed and spread
on the surface, and Diesel rollers ran up and down. And the
last thing was a two-inch layer of finer material, which was
the finishing touch.

A short ceremony was held at the junction near the Eastern
Main Road in Barataria for the opening of the road to civilians.
Government officials and United States officers attended, as
well as a few people from the cream of Port of Spain's society.
A thin blue ribbon across the road was cut, and it was chris-
tened the Churchill-Roosevelt Highway.

The fame of it spread throughout the length and breadth
of the island, and to the other islands in the West Indies, and
it became known as the best road in the Caribbean. To Trini-

dadians it was just "the Highway." Drivers left their usual routes to run on it; rich people took joy rides on it, delighting in the flow of speed, no bumps or cracks, as smooth as the sandy beach at Mayaro, a seaside resort. Donkey carts travelled on it, cyclists raced on it, a young coloured man took to exercising early in the morning, running for a half-mile on the highway. In the evenings lovers strolled on it. Farmers brought out their produce to sell at the sides of it. It ran inland from Barataria to the American base called Fort Read in the interior, and there was a constant flow of truck convoys of troops leaving the main road and getting on the highway, to and from the city and the base. From the airport visitors were driven on it, and they admired the scenery, sitting back and gliding along. The Americans put military policemen to patrol in jeeps and set a speed limit of thirty miles. But southbound vehicles took chances, it was almost impossible to resist accelerating on the highway, the car just sat down and glided, and the wind from across the fields whistled through the windows.

One day a donkey cart was coming out from one of the gravel roads in the back of the village. The old Indian driving didn't see the car shooting down the highway, and it struck the cart. The donkey was killed instantly, its blood splattered in the road.

Sometimes crapauds and small snakes were run over in the night as they crossed the highway from field to swamp.

CHAPTER ELEVEN

In April of 1944 the yellow and purple flowers of poui trees ran riot on the Northern Range under lifting war clouds, showing up in blobs on the brown hillside where farmers razed the land to plant new crops. It was the first sight for visitors as they entered the Gulf of Paria; it was the last for a detachment of Trinidad troops (of undisclosed strength) of the Caribbean Regiment as they left the island for an unknown destination. They eventually turned up in Italy and came under fire from bombing attacks. They had a good time with the Italian girls and wrote home about it. The Civil Defence Force was demobilized, and testing of air-raid sirens ceased. Private cars were zoned to their counties on account of the acute tyre shortage; buses and trains were the only means of transportation, and Trinidadians began to queue up for things. The government set a limit of one dollar and twenty cents on the cost of meals at restaurants so people wouldn't eat so much. With the completion of work on the American bases labour returned to agriculture, food production increased, a record rice crop was reaped, and as far as labour economics were concerned things looked better. The Education Board delegated power to the Director of Education to make all appointments for teachers; compulsory education, requiring every

child of schoolable age who resided within two miles of a
school to attend, was introduced. In Port of Spain, a poui tree
in front of the Red House in St. Vincent Street bore an abun-
dance of flowers; they fell, spinning in the air to the sidewalk,
and passers-by crushed them under their feet. A keskidee
stood on the branch of a tree outside of the magistrate's court
and distracted a man who was giving evidence at a murder
trial. A native raped a girl in the Queen's Park Savannah one
dark night and was imprisoned for five years; everyone who
had time to spare turned up in court to hear the case. Allied
servicemen flocked in the streets of the city. The officers sat
in the Country Club, or the other clubs which had been built
to entertain them, and sipped rum punches and gossiped with
the social strata. The privates and corporals and sergeants
looked for whores in George Street. One night a fight broke
out at Green Corner, where streets and prostitutes and idlers
met, between American servicemen and natives. A sailor had
been with a prostitute and refused to pay, and hell broke loose
suddenly, with bottles and stones hurling in the air and people
screaming and running all over the place. A native ran into a
parlour and climbed over the counter and snatched two bottles
of Coca-Cola, and the attendant didn't stop him. The native
crept up behind the sailor and with a seemingly careless throw
tossed a bottle above the sailor's head. Just as it was descending
to hit the sailor he hurled the other, and the two met just above
the American's head and shattered. It was perfectly timed,
those who saw were amazed. The sailor dropped to his knees,
bleeding from shrapnel. By the time the military police arrived
in jeeps everything was quiet. There were places out of bounds
to the American servicemen, and whenever they went there
they were beaten by the natives. The people liked their
money and carefreeness but hated them all the same. Too much

Yankee man leave Trinidad girl with child and go away. Hooliganism soared, and people kept off the streets at night.

Tiger began to build his house after he was finished with the road. He built slowly, on the same site as the hut. He dug four holes, with the hut in the centre, and he filled them up with concrete for the posts. That alone took him two months, working by himself in silence. Everything was past and gone, there was only the house to build now. To watch it grow, like a plant, brick by brick.

He sent Urmilla and Chandra to his parents in Chaguanas, saying that she needed plenty rest, and she couldn't get it in Barataria. She protested, as he expected, saying that she wanted to stay with him and help to build the house, but he laughed.

"What you could do? No, man, I want you to go. The rest and the change will do you good, you will forget all what happen, and by the time you come back the house will finish halfway. You go see."

"But who go cook for you and wash you clothes?"

"If you stop to worry bout all of that, you will never go. Don't bother bout me. I go eat anything, and wash the dirty clothes myself."

"You want me to tell them bout everything what happen, Tiger?"

"If you want. It don't matter much, if you tell them or if you don't tell them. Everything finish; it can't change anything."

"But what bout work? What you will do, now the road finish and you get lay off?"

"Don't worry, man. Plenty things to do around the village, I could help people weed garden and clean yard, and sell milk from the cow. You mustn't worry bout me when you go down Chaguanas. Go and see all your friends, and have a good time, and forget Barataria. If *mai* or *bap* ask for me, or any of my friends, tell them I keeping fine. Tell them I might come back just now too, when I finish some business up here."

"Is when I must come back, Tiger? How long to stay?"

"I go let you know. I might come to meet you. You better pack up a few things right away, today. If you stop to think too much, you does change your mind, so you better go one time. Take enough money with you, you know. Don't go down there and make them believe that we poor and begging. Buy something and carry for them, and don't ask them for no money. Take enough so you won't run short."

Sometimes he went out on the highway at night and walked, watching the cars fly with scarcely a sound, headlights playing far ahead, in bamboo trees when the road curved. Sometimes he would meet someone he knew, driving a donkey cart.

"Aaye, who dat dere? Tiger?"

"Yes, man."

"Wat you doam dis side so late in de night? Yuh not fraid jumbie?"

"Just taking a walk, man. Where you going?"

"Going city side, market, provision. Sell early in morning time."

"You have room on the cart?"

"You want goam city? Come den, jump up, let we talk. Ah glad for company, dis road too dark and lonely. Ah hear yuh loseam one boy child? Him born dead?"

"That was a long time ago."

"How long? Two, three month, callam dat long? Me haveam four boy child"—proudly—"all big man, work, drive taxi, plant garden side."

"But how it is, they never think about doing anything else besides that? They never want to go to college in Port of Spain, or go away and study lawyer and doctor?"

"Who time go away? For wat? Liveam country side, happy. No trouble. Belly full, nice wife, plenty boy child dem have too, why go way?"

"It have plenty things besides that. If they go to school, they could learn to read and write, and get good jobs in the town."

Jaggernauth guffawed. He lived in the back of the village, in Jogee Road, which ran between Barataria and San Juan. He had heard of Tiger educating himself and thought it a waste of time.

"Why you not go way, eh? You tellum oder people go, but you stay dis side."

"One day I will go away," Tiger said steadily, watching a part of the highway he remembered working on.

"You goam city side, yuh want to be in government, politic? Dat's why yuh study? Want to fight for Indian rights?"

"Everybody rights, not only Indian."

"Chuts! Indian must come first! Yuh not like dat one Ramroop at all. Who time voting come, Ramroop come village side and make big speech, say he help Indian if we put him government side. Him give every man five, ten dollar. Him send car to carry men dat side to vote. Big pretty car. We vote, and Ramroop get councillor. Two, three time he come village side, everybody say, 'Look, Mr. Ramroop come!' We say, no water, no work, no electric light. He say, all right, he go fixam. He say Indian must come first."

"I notice water still scarce, plenty people still out of work, and you still burning lamp."

"But he trying hard for we Indian! Who time poor man like you get government side? You not have house, you not have land, you not have money. All my son haveam no education, but dem all have more money dan you!"

The donkey cart took two hours to reach Port of Spain, and he sometimes stayed the night, sleeping on bags of provisions on the sidewalk. Just waiting for something to happen, that was all. Things happened, all you had to do was wait. One night he thought of going with a prostitute, but she asked for too much money. He thought how he had sweated to earn, and he laughed in her face, and she called him a cheap coolie dog. What did it matter what people called you? It was what you was inside that count. So much poor people huddle up on the pavement sleeping, because the one poor house in the city overcrowded. So much American and other soldiers and sailors all over the place, like if the war was in Trinidad. He went into the most expensive cinemas, just waiting for someone to challenge him, to say, What yuh doing here, coolie? And he drifted about the streets of the city, ready to explode if anyone dared to question his right. Late in the night he returned to the village and slept restlessly. I should talk to Joe Martin and Rita, I ain't talk to them since that night. It not their fault, is nobody fault but mine. Why I so stupid? The two of them is the best friends I ever had. I too shame.

But the sun burned away resolutions of the night. Brick by brick he built, doing all he could, leaving what he couldn't do alone for the last, because he was keeping away from the villagers he knew. They would only talk about it if I go in the shop. They would say how they sorry to hear. But what is the use of that? They won't mean no harm, but just to hear them talk will make me remember, and I want to forget.

He did odd jobs in the village, keeping out of his friends' ways as much as possible. He didn't want to go on spending money, he had worked too hard for it to just trickle through his fingers, and eventually he took to selling milk.

He didn't know how to approach Rita about the milk. He decided he would just fill a bottle and leave it there on her back step where she could see it easily. If in the morning it was still there, well, he would just have to forget her as a customer.

But in the morning the bottle had been emptied and washed clean. He looked for Rita, he had an uncomfortable feeling she was watching him, but he couldn't see her. He felt pleased about the milk; every day now he left a bottle. And when it was the ending of the week, and he was wondering how he would ask her for the money, he found it under the bottle on the step.

It was Rita who hastened a reconciliation. One morning, as he was milking the cow, she looked over the hibiscus fence and shouted, "Wat de hell yuh mean by leaving stale milk for me yesterday? Ah mad to bust de bottle on yuh head!"

"But, Rita, you startle me!" he exclaimed, upsetting the pail of milk.

"Yuh better make sure is fresh milk yuh leave dis morning, dat is all," she said.

He always made sure he gave her the best; a smile came to his face, and he felt like he wanted to cry for no reason. When Rita saw it her voice softened and she cried, "Tiger!" and he swallowed a lump in his throat.

It was Rita who cried, and laughed at the same time, cursing her tears.

"Yuh know it wasn't my fault, Tiger! Ah try me best, so help me God, but wat is to is, must is. It hurt me to tink yuh blaming me in yuh mind—"

"I not blaming you, Rita. I was a damn fool, is all my fault. All the time, I did want to come over and see you and Joe, and say I sorry. But I can't make up my mind."

She let loose a barrage of questions. "Way Urmilla? Yuh send she way? Ah miss she too bad, man, me and she uses to have some good times together wen you and Joe gone to work. Wen she coming back? But wat happening and ting? So long we ain't talk! Wat job yuh doing now? Like yuh not working dese days, Ah does see yuh working on de house. It coming good, man, but yuh can't build dat by yuhself. So wat happening? Yuh' know dey lay Joe off de base? Yes, man. But he get ah job wid de railway in Port of Spain."

Tiger managed to get in a word. "Urmilla gone Chaguanas for a holiday. I don't know how long she going to stay. For a long time, maybe."

"So nobody to cook or do anyting for yuh! Look how thin yuh getting! Like yuh ain't had a good curry for a long time! Ah cooking curry today, Ah go keep some for yuh."

"Is all right, don't trouble yourself—"

"Shut yuh big mouth! So wat yuh doing dese days? Wat happening? Tall Boy did tell me to tell yuh not to forget yuh owe him some money still, but I did tell him dat you and me not talking, and he laugh and say dat dat always happening, but I tell him dis time is de last time, dat we done for good. And look how we talking now! A—a, but, boy, yuh hear how everybody saying dat Ma Mary is ah *soucouyant?* Yuh know she? She living by ninth street, she does take in washing. Dey say she sucking everybody baby blood, is ah good ting Chandra not here! Last night dey find bloodstain all in she yard—"

Still, friends don't fill up all the spaces in your heart. They can't undo anything what happen already. Joe is the only one now, with poor old Sookdeo dead and gone. I friendly with Boysie, but he going away after the war, and I might never see him again. Is only Joe next door to talk to. Talk about what? Well, how we used to talk about plenty things, about politics and thing. Talk about work. Talk about the house. What everybody else does talk about. A man must have a friend to talk to, otherwise he come like some of them old people talking to themself!

The dry season lingered. On the Northern Range green turned to a sullen brown. Dry leaves fluttered in the wind, falling on the lawns in the city parks, scurrying on the sidewalks, spinning spiral in circular breezes and dropping in the drains. Children tried to catch yellow leaves before they touched the ground, for luck. The sun blazed in the sky as if rain had never fallen. In the bases Americans walked about in merinos and shorts, and bathed often in the sea. But middle-class natives working in the city continued to wear their ties and jackets, anxious to keep their position in society. In Barataria the farmers worked on the land as usual. Only the highway itself was a reminder of the past; they lifted their heads at zooming traffic and went back to work. It was commonplace to see vehicles speeding through the fields now. A tale reached their ears from Tunapuna, a distant village, where the highway ran. How one evening, a car "eat up de road doing ah easy sixty." How the military police saw it and gave chase, for it was moving far above the speed limit. It was a maroon convertible Chevrolet coupé, and the jeep drove it off the road, and one of the Americans demanded to see the licence of the driver. It was a white woman driving, her husband sat next to her. How, when they looked behind the car to see the number, they saw a crown painted in gold. How they scrambled back and saluted the Governor of the colony and his wife and drove the jeep down into the drain to allow them to proceed. And how the natives laughed! They said, "Dat is one time yuh cuddn't do anyting, Joe!" And the Americans grinned and drove off. From lip to lip the tale went, and the incident was discussed in all the rumshops, but no one knew if the Governor or his wife related it in their circle.

The Indian summer came with a few light showers. Tiger's house was going higher. At length he had had to seek assistance from his friends, and on Sundays they dropped around to lend a hand. They didn't work according to a plan, but they measured here and there, and looked at the house Joe lived in for guidance. Joe himself lifted a brick or two, and Rita abused him loudly in front of everybody, saying how he wouldn't clean his own yard or clear away the bush, but helped Tiger to build his house, as if he had a share in it. And Joe said building a house was a different thing, that there was something standing up for years after it was built, but if he swept the yard the damn place would get nasty again, so what was the use of doing it? He said Henry should do that sort of thing, and he used to get the little boy busy every Saturday morning before allowing him to run off and play. Tiger bought a good supply of rum for he knew it encouraged them to work, and they drank while working, and made jokes, and said how they all had shares in the house, and when it was completed they would move in with their wives and children.

The year waned. In Port of Spain a trigger-happy sentry in the Home Guard shouted who goes there and when he didn't get a reply he shot an old Negro wharf stevedore one night. Two coloured and three white girls had abortions. In the hills the land slid when the rains began and buried a house and three people. Tall Boy's wife had another baby, a girl this time. Urmilla returned from Chaguanas. They all loved Chandra so much they begged her to leave the baby for a few weeks, and she came back alone, in the government railway bus.

She was surprised and happy to see how the house had progressed. The hut was demolished and parts used for the erection of a bigger kitchen. There was galvanize on the roof of the house, and it had flooring, so they could live in it while it was being completed. She walked comfortably in shoes now and wore her sari with a touch of pride. The holiday had done her well. Not that she had rested a great deal. She had had to cook for the whole family and help in the house, cleaning. But the change of environment, as Tiger put it, "bring back the colour in your face, and learn you to live again."

"So what we going to do now, Tiger? Your father ask you if you want to come back and work in the canefield, he say big sugar crop this year, plenty work for everybody."

"You think I going back to work in canefields again? Not if is the last thing in the world to do! We have plenty money still, so don't worry. It hard to plan for the future, things does happen and change everything. Let everything go as it going, we will see later."

He showed her two beds of lettuce he had planted at the side of the house, "to keep my hand in practice, just in case I have to go back to gardening."

"I too glad we make back friend with Rita and Joe," Urmilla said. "When I tell them home what happen, they blame Rita and say is she fault. We had a big quarrel, because I stick up for she. Tiger, it just like the first time we come up here to live, eh? You remember? But now we have a house, and more money. We go start all over again, and this time we won't make so much mistake, eh, Tiger?"

"You don't start over things in life," he said wisely, "you just have to go on from where you stop. It not as if you born all over again. Is the same life."

CHAPTER TWELVE

Precensorship of papers of passengers travelling to England from Trinidad ceased in January 1945, and it was announced by the government that identity cards were no longer necessary. The next month the Home Guard was disbanded, and those who were in it held parties in the restaurants and got drunk, and one man was run over by an American truck in Park Street. Gradually restrictive legislation slackened. V-E and V-J Day celebrations were marked by patriotic demonstrations and wild merriment; steel bands, growing in the war years, took to the streets for the first time, and pandemonium reigned as Trinidadians were allowed to indulge in two days of Carnival, an annual festival which was held up when war broke out. There were fights between civilians and service personnel, and steel bands clashed, pelting bottles and stones and wielding sticks. Later on in the year censorship was stopped altogether, motorcar zoning abolished, and restaurants were allowed to serve meals late in the evening. In the sugar and oil industries wage agreements were signed, but many people were still out of work, and labourers marched in the streets with placards, and a delegation visited the Governor, seeking relief. The legislature adopted a motion providing for increased benefits under the workmen's compensation ordinance. In San Fernando a man appeared in court and registered his one hundred and forty-fifth conviction in three years. He had jacked up a car parked in front of a cinema and stolen the tyres. A Pan-American seaplane crashed and twenty-three out of thirty passengers were drowned. The report of the West Indies Royal Commission was released for publication; the demand for copies was five times greater than the quantity available. The cost of living rose to 200 points, and it was a difficult thing to get butter and saltfish in the shops.

The morning of the day peace was officially announced radios said that the Prime Minister of England would make a definite statement in the evening, but nobody waited for it. Steel-band players east of the Dry River tuned their pans and drums, people rushed excitedly about the streets, and Joe Martin dashed to Barataria.

"Allyuh hear wat happen? Peace declare! No more war! Oh lordy oh! Is fire in town tonight! Big fete all over de place! Me, I going back now, gul, put some food on de table dere for me right away! Steel band will make ruckshun in town tonight. Come, do quick, don't stand up dere looking at me so! If yuh coming to town, look out for fight. Which part yuh hide de rum? Call Tiger and Urmilla, let we fire one! Oh gawd! Is fire in town! Do quick, gul, do quick!"

"Tiger, Tiger!" Boysie called. "Yuh not going to town? Come and go wid me, man! Ah hear fete for so in town! Man, peace declare! No more war!"

"Wait for me, come inside and sit down," Tiger said and hurried to dress.

"Every time you going to town I asking you to carry me go with you and you saying no," Urmilla said. "Well, carry me now, nar, I want to see the celebrations too."

"Look, girl, if I carry you it go be trouble, man. I go have to look out for you. Not today! You don't hear people gone mad in town? Not today, man, really. If you want, go with Rita."

"Man, Rita have she own friend in town, I don't want to humbug she."

"Well, stay with Chandra then."

"Cook dinner for you?" she called as he went out with Boysie.

"Yes," he flung over his shoulder, "but I don't know when I coming back!"

The streets were jammed with bands of masqueraders dressed in old costumes which had been put away for the war. Crowds jumped up to the music of steel orchestras, and everywhere there was gaiety and song and laughter and shouting and yelling.

It did not take them very long to get drunk and join the revelry. They pulled their shirts out of their trousers and clasped each other round the waist and jumped in a band.

Suddenly Boysie shouted, "Look, Joe band! Look, Joe dere, beating de pingpong! Let we go in he band, man!"

They ran across the road and waited for the band to come nearer. They screamed, "Joe! Joe!" But it was impossible for him to hear them in the din. Joe was having the time of his life; it was his first public appearance as a steel-band player, and he was pounding out calypsoes and shaking his body to the rhythm.

Seasons come and go quickly in Trinidad, but always the sun shines and the birds sing and the flowers bloom, and the wind blows down from the Northern Range to cool the land.

The house was almost completed, and Tiger gave Urmilla money and told her to buy what she wanted to furnish it. She and Rita went to town on a spending spree.

Boysie had booked passage for New York, and one morning

he met Tiger in Tall Boy's shop and showed him the passport.

"So you really going, eh, Boysie? You make up your mind? You leaving Trinidad?"

"Yes, boy, dis land too hard. Plenty money in de States. If ever Ah come back, Ah go be ah rich man. But how bout you, Tiger? Wat yuh doing dese days? Yuh working yet? De house finish building?"

"I might get a job with the railways in Port of Spain, where Joe working. He tell me to go and see the foreman, but I ain't gone yet."

"Well, have ah drink on me, nar, if yuh not too busy. Let we sit down here and talk. Why yuh don't go way too? Ain't yuh have money?"

"How you want me to leave my wife and child and house and go away just so?"

"Man, yuh cud send dem Chaguanas! Yuh cud sell de house and de cow, and go way and study and come back lawyer!"

"The way you say it, it sound easy. And to tell you the truth, boy, it had a time when I was thinking of doing that, yes. But it have plenty other things to think about, Boysie. A man just can't take up heself and do this and do that."

"If Ah stop to tink too much, Ah bet yuh Ah don't go no place! But yuh have to take chances in life sometimes. Look at me, Ah don't know wat Ah going into, but Ah still going."

"Yes, but you ain't have no family to bother about. You on your own, you could do what you like. It different with me. It ain't always a man does be able to do the things he want to do. Is when the boat sailing? If I have time I could come and see you go on board."

"Is next week Monday. I cud pass around by yuh wen Ah ready to go, and we cud go to town together. Listen, man, wat yuh doing tonight?"

"Nothing much."

"Well, how bout dropping round by me? Couple of de boys coming, we having ah little party. Is freeness."

"About what time so?"

"Any time after dinner, man. Ah looking out for yuh."

Sunlight glared on the asphalt of the highway, waves of heat rose and shimmered, and he walked on the grass at the side, for the road was too hot.

He called out to the farmers. "Rajnauth! How the ricefield going?"

"Aaye, Tiger! Ah hear yuh was drunk in town de oder day!"

"But how you mean? Peace declare, I must get drunk!"

"But tings still hard to get in de shop! Prices still high!"

"You can't expect everything to come back as it was so quick, man. It will take a long time."

Afterwards, thinking of his remarks as cars whizzed past and put wind on his face, it seemed to him as if he was always saying the same things, asking the same questions. Wat happening dere, boy? I all right, man. How you? How the garden going? There was too much of this sameness, all over, in the gardens, in the shops, in the village streets. What difference did anything make? It seemed no one knew that a battle had been won, that peace had been declared. They still went to work in the fields, the sun still shone, Tall Boy's shop was still there, they said the same things, over and over, day after day. He would go home and Urmilla would show him the furniture she bought. They would eat dinner; he would sit and read, or they would talk old things. Plenty things happened, but nothing new. The story he had written about the highway he had posted to the *Trinidad Guardian* short-story contest, he hadn't got a reply yet. Not that he expected any success; he just posted it because he felt all his labour would have been in vain if someone else didn't see it. Only for Boysie things would be new. Going to a big country, where the houses so high you can't see the tops, and they have trains that does run under the ground. One city alone so big, you could lose the whole of Trinidad in it!

He considered going back to the canefields in Chaguanas, but the thought of it made him laugh aloud. He broke a blade of grass and put it in his mouth.

Overhead a cloud fled the sun, moving in a swift breeze.

"Now is a good time to plant corn," he muttered, gazing up at the sky.

Firebrands

Sahle Sellassie

A tale of two brothers in the Ethiopia of the early 1970s. Bezuneh, the elder, is a gentle giant of a man, honest and hard-working in a corrupt world. Worku, the younger, is a hot-headed student, eager to sweep away the system and set the downtrodden masses free.

As the people's resentment against their overlords seethes and festers, Bezuneh reaches his own boiling point when he is unjustly sacked. Imprisoned for his murderous assault upon his boss, he is freed after the revolution has overthrown the ruling class. But how far has the system *really* changed?

Sahle Sellassie's third novel is a forceful and realistic story set against the background of the dramatic events of 1974.

ISBN 0 582 64243 4

Muriel at Metropolitan

Miriam Tlali

Muriel is a Black South African who gets a job at Metropolitan Radio, a furniture store in the heart of Johannesburg. Unwillingly she finds herself taking part in the exploitation of her own people, the Black customers who are tempted by 'buy now pay later' bargains and then threatened when they fall behind.

Muriel's personal narrative of day to day life in the store reveals her growing resentment of the petty snubs and indignities unthinkingly dealt out by the white staff. Gradually we come to recognise that the store is a virtual microcosm of South African society under apartheid.

Miriam Tlali's novel, based on her own experiences, describes simply and without sensationalism the plight of the South African Black struggling to find and keep a place in a society where white is always right.

ISBN 0 582 64232 9

Violence

Festus Iyayi

The worst thing that can happen to a man is to wake up each morning not only hungry but with no means of satisfying his hunger or that of his wife. Idemudia's unremitting struggle for survival in a city offering cruel contrasts between direst poverty and ostentatious wealth almost destroys him, his health and his marriage. The bond between him and his wife Adisa is stretched, strained, battered and betrayed, yet from their sufferings miraculously emerge a deeper insight and a closer unity.

This is Festus Iyayi's first novel, written from his own observations of conditions existing in his native Nigeria.

ISBN 0 582 64247 7